Karin Ellis

Applying for jobs in Norway

*How to crack the hidden codes –
a step-by-step guide*

Copyright © Karin Ellis
Latest revision: 14th August 2021
v1.8

Ellis Culture
www.ellisculture.com

All rights reserved.
This book, or any portion thereof may not be reproduced or used in any manner whatsoever without the express written permission of the author, except for the use of brief quotations where the author's name is mentioned.

Any copyrighted material is reproduced under the fair use doctrine,
or with the permission of the copyright holder.

ISBN: 1985196751
ISBN-13: 978-1985196759

Other books written by Karin Ellis:
Working with Norwegians

Norwegian editions:
Kunsten å arbeide med nordmenn
Kunsten å søke jobb i Norge
Flerkulturelle arbeidsplasser

Other editions:
Menas susirasti darbą Norvegijoje (Lithuanian)
Искусство поиска работы в Норвегии (Russian)

www.ellisculture.com/en/books

CONTENTS

INTRODUCTION 1

1 PREPARATIONS 7

    1.1   Checklist for job-seeking in Norway 8
    1.2   Getting NOKUT recognition 9
    1.3   Job portals 11
    1.4   Job announcement 14

2 MAKING THE APPLICATION DOCUMENTS 17

    2.1   Writing the application letter 19
    2.2   Writing the CV 25
    2.3   Testimonials 31

3 EXAMPLES 33

    3.1   Questions for the phone call 33
    3.2   Temporary position becoming permanent 35
    3.3   Application letter samples 36
    3.4   CV samples 48
    3.5   Testimonial sample 62
    3.6   Statements to be avoided 63
    3.7   Examples of good statements 66

4 THE JOB INTERVIEW 67

    4.1   Preparations 69
    4.3   Selling yourself at the right level 73
    4.4   Discussing your strengths and weaknesses 74
    4.5   Questions asked by employers 74
    4.6   Questions you could ask 77
    4.7   Cases to test your skills 78
    4.8   What else to be prepared for 79
    4.9   Cultural aspects in the interview 80

5	WHAT EMPLOYERS LOOK FOR	83
	5.1 Selection of candidates	83
	5.2 Results from an employer survey	88

6	GETTING STARTED IN NORWAY	89
	6.1 The easiest ways into the job market	89
	6.2 A possible door opener for the dream job	91
	6.3 Some final advice	93
	6.4 Getting the job offer	97
	6.5 Salary negotiations before accepting a job offer	99
	6.6 If you did not get the job	100
	6.7 Starting your own business in Norway	101
	6.8 Trade unions	102

7	PERSONALITY TESTS	105
	7.1 Why personality tests are used	106
	7.2 Types of tests	107
	7.3 Tips for the tests	108

CLOSING NOTE	111
REFERENCES	113
ABOUT THE AUTHOR	116

DEDICATION

For my husband, Ingvar, my beloved soul-mate,
for your patience and support.

ACKNOWLEDGEMENTS

A big thank you to:

Neil Wright for your enthusiastic proofreading,
for challenging my English and helping me improve my texts.

Halyna Lystvak for patiently reading my book,
as always with your sharp eye for details and
for finding the errors that were missed by others.

Anna Kuzmenko for making the front and back cover
as well the illustrations in this book,
crisp and clear and always to my liking.

Recruiters at universities, municipalities,
companies and temporary agencies in Norway
for sharing their experiences and
providing valuable input for this book

INTRODUCTION

Background

I hope you will enjoy this book on how to apply for jobs in Norway. My name is Karin Ellis. I am a Norwegian living in Bergen on the west coast of Norway.

I have 30 years' experience, with approximately 20 years in leadership positions, from large Norwegian companies with an international presence. I have worked on projects with people from all over the world, and have always been interested in learning as much as possible about different cultures.

In 2011 I decided to take the big step of moving away from a well-paid management position and venturing into the unknown where I started my own company, Ellis Culture, in order to develop and conduct intercultural training full time.

Among our most popular training courses are **Working with Norwegians** and **Applying for jobs in Norway.**

I have conducted **Working with Norwegians** for several thousand people in companies and universities, both in Norway and in a large number of other countries too.

I first started collecting the content for an **Applying for jobs in Norway** training course in 2012, when I was asked to develop this course for a large Norwegian university. We discussed in particular how this course should focus on the common mistakes made by foreigners. Since then I have gathered input from several recruiters in Norway. Some of them have read parts of this book and provided valuable feedback and comments before it was published.

During my 30 years in different workplaces I have been both a job-seeker and a recruiter. I have also read research reports on this topic. This book is therefore based on my own experience, research, talking to Norwegian employers/recruiters, as well as on the experiences of thousands of non-Norwegian job-seekers in my courses.

In 2017 I published my first book, **Working with Norwegians**, on Amazon. The book was written in English to reach the widest possible audience, and I was soon asked to translate it into Norwegian by foreigners in Norway who did not speak English. It was published in Norwegian in 2018 under the title **Kunsten å arbeide med nordmenn**, also on Amazon. You may read more about my first book on www.ellisculture.com/en/books.

Goals of this book

There are many Norwegian books about how to apply for jobs, however this one is quite unique. Written specifically for English speakers who did not grow up in Norway, it will guide you through the job-seeking process step-by-step, and help you crack the hidden codes in the Norwegian job market.

It will give you tips on how to deal with the additional challenge of being a foreign job-seeker in the Norwegian job market and will hopefully help you to be better prepared when seeking jobs

Introduction

- Learn the particulars of the Norwegian job-seeking process
- Learn how to sell yourself to Norwegian employers
- Learn about typical mistakes made by non-Norwegians
- Boost your awareness of what Norwegian employers look for and what they expect

You will find out how to sell your personal qualities and competencies in a culturally acceptable way, and also discover what Norwegian employers prioritise when they select their candidates.

Job-seeking is a very demanding process

You should bear in mind that job-seeking can be so time consuming that it is often comparable to having a full time job. As such, you need to be mentally prepared for the ups and downs (and there will usually be more downs than ups). It is therefore important to focus on your strengths and try not to lose faith. At the same time you should reflect upon what you can learn from the downs and start planning what you will do differently next time.

When you are upset because you have not got the job you have applied for, you should take a break and take extra good care of yourself for a day or two. In this respite, you should do something you enjoy doing and perhaps treat yourself to something extra nice. I would also recommend that you try to get out into the fresh air and get some exercise every day whilst applying for jobs.

It is also important to be systematic and goal-oriented. Do not let excuses get in the way of calling the recruiters. Ensure you are physically active and maintain a normal day rhythm by getting up early and going to bed at a reasonably time.

It is particularly demanding applying for a first job in Norway. Norwegians also struggle with this, since most employers seem to look for people with some work experience. Whilst applying for jobs, you should also focus on building your networks.

Trends in the Norwegian job market

The Norwegian economy is fundamentally solid with low unemployment rates, profitable companies and solid banks. The unemployment rate in Norway has generally been among the lowest in Europe, even in periods of financial crisis and recession in the global labor market.

Statistics from the Norwegian Labour and Welfare Administration (NAV) have shown that many employers are unable to find qualified applicants, and that they often have to recruit a candidate with lower qualifications than they had hoped for. On average, in 10% of the recruitment instances Norwegian employers failed to find qualified candidates for their positions, and in 6% of the instances they had to recruit a candidate with lower qualifications than they were hoping for. In the following occupations, it has recently been difficult to find enough qualified labour:

- Healthcare professionals (doctors, nurses)
- Teachers
- Engineers (IT, chemistry, electronics, mechanics, civil engineers)
- Electricians, welders, mechanics
- Technicians (quality controllers, technical experts)
- Professional drivers
- Project managers, lawyers and researchers
- Salespeople
- Construction workers (builders, carpenters, brick layers)
- Industrial workers (production, machine operators)

Therefore, there has therefore been some labour immigration to Norway. However, the challenge of finding work should not be underestimated. It can be difficult for non-Norwegian job-seekers to get a job. Especially the first job in Norway is difficult to get. In Norway, there are many jobseekers with higher education, but not many with work experience.

Those who struggle most to get a job in Norway are young people without work experience, those with short or little education, as well as non-Norwegian jobseekers. For some employers, it may seem like a safer choice to employ Norwegian candidates because they feel that it will be more predictable when it comes to the need for training and adaptation. This unconscious bias is more common in small and medium-sized businesses, and in particular in those that are more traditional or family-run. Employers in the public sector, municipalities, academia, research, high-tech companies, hotels, restaurants, bars, many shops, as well as start-ups are less likely to have such prejudices. Companies that already have a multicultural workforce have broken the threshold of hiring people from other cultures. Examples are Ikea and the post companies.

There are regional differences in the structure of employment in Norway. In the large cities like Oslo, Bergen and Trondheim, many people work within financial and business services. Industries such as oil, gas, energy and fisheries account for a large share in the coastal regions of southern Norway, while public services and fisheries are the dominant sectors in the north. There is less regional variation in other sectors like building, construction, health care and teaching.

It is generally easier to find service related jobs in Oslo than in other Norwegian cities.

Unemployment benefit while looking for a job in Norway

EEA countries are the EU member states as well as Norway, Iceland and Liechtenstein. EEA regulations coordinate the law regulating rights to social insurance in the various member states in order to ensure continuous coverage. The main objective of these regulations is to ensure that you are not deprived of any benefits that you are entitled to. Being employed in Norway entitles you and your immediate family to the same rights as Norwegian citizens.

It is possible for people from EEA countries who are entitled to unemployment benefit in their home country to have their benefits transferred to Norway. If this is relevant for you, you should contact the local unemployment office in your home country and take the necessary steps to transfer your benefits, by filling in a form before departing for Norway.

If you become unemployed in Norway without fulfilling the requirements for unemployment benefit here, you may request that any rights that you have earned in another EEA country be transferred to Norway.

The contact information for NAV EEA Unemployment Benefit is listed in the reference section in the end of the book (2).

I collect beautiful stones.
Every time I fall,
I take one down with me.
They will become an upward staircase.

Kjersti Aune

1 PREPARATIONS

Before you start reading this book I would like to give you the most important piece of advice: start learning Norwegian!

I meet so many foreigners in Norway and many of them have not bothered to learn Norwegian because they have not known how long they would be here, or they did not think it was necessary because most Norwegians speak English so well.

I can safely say that you will never feel like a first rate employee in the workplace until you master Norwegian. There will be meetings and occasions when people revert to Norwegian and you will feel left out.

As an example, this is some feedback I received after writing my first book **Working with Norwegians**:

"I am struggling with not being able to communicate in Norwegian at work. When I accepted the job it was clearly stated it was not a requirement but now I don't feel like that anymore. I feel like for some of my colleagues it is hard to understand why I don't speak it and it is making me feel very uncomfortable. I really wish I could communicate in Norwegian at work."

1.1   Checklist for job-seeking in Norway

1. Employer
2. Position
3. Yourself
4. Motivation
5. Application

1. Knowledge of the employer
Try to gather as much information about the employer as you can. What is their strategy, their products/services and challenges? This will enable you to write the best possible application by targeting it for the role and company. You will find tips about this in chapters 1.3, 1.4, 3.1 and 4.1.

2. Understanding the position
Try to find out what the position really entails, what skills and qualities are important for managing the tasks, and what kind of person the employer is looking for. There are tips about this in chapters 1.3 and 3.1.

3. Knowledge about yourself
What do you find interesting and motivating? What kind of job and tasks will motivate you? What are you like as a person, and how are you perceived by others? How could your experience and personal qualities be valuable for this particular employer? More about this in chapters 2.1 and 7.3.

4. Finding your inner motivation
This is the most important part, and a crucial test to pass in being selected. If you have gone through the previous steps of this list, you will be able to come across as well prepared and genuinely motivated for the position. There are tips about this in chapters 2, 3 and 4.

5. Adapting your application
If you have gone through the steps above, it will be easier to adapt your application towards each employer and position you apply for, ref. tips in chapters 2 and 3.

1.2 Getting NOKUT recognition

NOKUT (the Norwegian Agency for Quality Assurance in Education) is an independent expert body under the Ministry of Education and Research. NOKUT's tasks are, among other things, to recognise foreign higher education and a few vocational educations from five EU countries.

A general recognition of your education is not mandatory, but it is recommended.

NOKUT`s recognition decisions are based on comparing the foreign educational system against the Norwegian degree structure (i.e. Bachelor, Master's or PhD).

Please note however that this is not an evaluation of the academic content of your education, nor a subject specific recognition; it is a general recognition of level and scope. You should also note that for regulated professions, it is mandatory to obtain authorisation/recognition of your professional qualifications by the competent authority, responsible for this particular profession. You will find information about the application process and recognition authorities by selecting your profession on the NOKUT webpage (8).

If your profession is not in NOKUT's list, it may be because it requires no specific recognition before you can start working in Norway. Positions requiring engineers, economists, social workers, journalists, beauticians and painters/decorators, for example, are not regulated and do not require recognition or authorisation.

The NOKUT recognition may help you to establish yourself in the Norwegian job market and may also help your future employers with salary placement.

You can also submit this recognition when applying for jobs in professions that are not regulated. It is up to the individual employers if they require you to have recognition from NOKUT or not.

Getting a NOKUT recognition of your education is free of charge; however, the documents which must be submitted (such as diplomas, certificates, transcripts of grades and proofs of name changes etc.) must be translated into English, Norwegian, or other Scandinavian languages, which may be costly. You will find complete information on documentation requirements on NOKUT's website (8).

NOKUT also has a recognition of certificate of apprenticeships for non-regulated professions from Poland, Germany and the Baltic countries. If you have such a certificate it is recommended that you apply for the recognition. If you have a certificate of apprenticeship from another country, you need to contact the local '*Fykeskommune*' to find out how you can achieve a Norwegian certificate of apprenticeship.

The processing time for NOKUT`s recognition is normally between two and four months, but can sometimes take longer.

Because the processing procedure may take time, you should first consider whether you wish to apply at all. If you do, I would advise you to apply as soon as possible while you are applying for jobs at the same time. You can always inform your potential employer about the ongoing application at NOKUT. The employer may contact NOKUT for information about your application.

NOKUT has a telephone service available two days a week and you may also send them an email with questions. The contact information is on their website (8).

1. Preparations

1.3 Job portals

The majority of vacancies in Norway are listed on the Internet. Many Norwegian companies have their own websites, and they sometimes advertise vacant positions that are not announced anywhere else. You may also find jobs in Norway on the website of the employment services in your home country.

NAV

NAV is the Norwegian Labour and Welfare Administration, which administers a third of the national budget through schemes such as unemployment benefit, work assessment allowance, sickness benefit, pensions, child benefit and cash-for-care benefit.

Their portal **www.nav.no** has a job search section. On this website you will find the most complete overview of vacant positions, and the list is constantly updated with new jobs.

NAV collects from job posting websites, municipal job boards and newspaper job advertisements, so it is a good starting point when looking for jobs in Norway.

The service is only in Norwegian, but since it is the largest portal for job vacancies in Norway, I would recommend that you overcome the language barrier and start using it. If you log in you can register your CV and customise your search, and set up automated searches where you will be notified by e-mail of job vacancies that meet your criteria.

There is a somewhat outdated tutorial (6) for NAV on the webpage 'My Little Norway' in the reference section of this book. This might be of some help to you.

Finn.no

Finn.no is the largest marketplace in Norway where you can buy or sell almost everything, and is very popular. There are two market areas in Finn related to jobs: "Jobb" and "Småjobber".

Whilst "Jobb" offers standard jobs on both a permanent and temporary basis; "Småjobber" primarily offers ad-hoc tasks such as gardening, repairs and cleaning, etc.

Finn is also only in Norwegian, but again I would recommend that you overcome the language barrier and start using it. Here you can also register your CV, customise your search, and set up an automated search where you will be notified by e-mail of job vacancies that meet your criteria.

Web pages for vacant positions

Workinnorway.no/en/ – official guide to work in Norway
Jobbsøk.no – Collection of jobs as well as useful information
Academicpositions.no – vacant positions in academia
Stillinger.no – Job recruitment
Jobb24.no – Database of job positions
JobbNorge.no – Recruitment portal
Adecco.no – Recruitment agency
Manpower.no – Recruitment agency
Offentlige-stillinger.com – Vacant positions in the public sector
Statsjobb.no – Governmental positions
ResearchGate.net – Research jobs
Medrec.no – Vacant positions within health care
Legejobber.no – Vacant positions for medical doctors
Skolejobb.no – Positions within the educational system
Pvs.no – Temporary jobs in schools and kindergartens
Teknojobb.no – Jobs within IT and communication
Jobbdirekte.no – Job application services
Bergen.kommune.no/jobb – Positions in the municipality of Bergen
Uib.no/stilling – Vacant positions at the University of Bergen
Journalisten.no – Positions in media
Mediabemanning.no – Recruitment for media and communication
Kommunikasjon.no/bransjen/ledige-stillinger – Vacant positions in media and communication
Jobb.tu.no/sok – *Teknisk ukeblad* (magazine) job announcements

Dnjobb.no – Vacant positions in the newspaper *Dagens Næringsliv*
Karrierestart.no – Starting point for job and career
Global.no/stillinger – Humanitarian aid work
Jobpilot.com – European career market
Monster.no – Norwegian career market
Careerjet.no – Jobs in Norway and the rest of the world
Projects-Abroad.no – Internship and voluntary work
Deltidsjobb.net – Part time jobs
Linkedin.com – Social network for job applicants

Useful information pages

NOKUT.no – Recognition of education and work experience
Skilledmigration.net – A study of international skilled migration
Utdanning.no – Overview of all fields of study and description of professions
Arbeidstilsynet.no – Information about the work environment and legislation
LO.no – The largest employee organisation in Norway
NHO.no – The largest organisation for companies in Norway
Skatteetaten.no – Information about tax for private persons and companies
Norge.no – Your guide to the governmental bodies in Norway
Altinn.no – Public reporting
Altinn.no/starte-og-drive – Portal for companies and founders, company information
Lovdata.no – Laws and legislation
Euraxess.no and **Euraxess.eu** – Support services for researchers
Forskning.no – Norwegian and international research news
Ec.europa.eu – Jobs and learning opportunities throughout Europe
Ssb.no/en/ – Statistics of Norway, i.e. salary statistics etc.

1.4   Job announcement

When you go through the job advertisement it is important to read it carefully. It would be helpful if you have a Norwegian friend or colleague who can go through it with you and read the nuances in the text.

For instance, when it comes to competence and personal qualities you should look for subtle nuances, e.g. must have (*må ha*) versus should have (*bør ha*) and if it says something is an advantage (*en fordel*) or desirable/preferable (*ønskelig/fordelaktig*).

Consider what is specified in the job announcement as a wish list from the employer, where they are describing the perfect candidate. They will probably not find anyone with all these qualities, so you should not lose courage and refrain from applying just because you lack some or many of them. The NAV statistics (3) in the introduction part of this book, states that 6% of Norwegian jobs are given to candidates with lower qualifications than the employers were hoping for.

How formal is the announcement? It may be hard for you to judge if it is in Norwegian, so this is where a Norwegian could help you. If the announcement has a formal tone, your application should also be quite formal. If it is more playful or creative then you can also be a bit more of the same.

You should also look for any requests for attachments. Usually attachments are not sent with the application, but if they ask for them then they should be included.

A complete application should consist of the following elements:

1. Application (cover) letter
2. CV
3. Attachments
   (certificates, testimonials, list of publications and similar)

It is important that you make a copy of the job announcement to your own computer or that you make a hardcopy of it by printing it out. Usually the job announcements are removed when the application deadline has been reached, and if you are invited for an interview it will be a disadvantage for you if you do not have the announcement.

It happened to me once and I was very uncomfortable when I was waiting for the interview to start because I could not remember exactly the information given and what they had asked for in the announcement.

Calling the recruiters

There are usually one or two contact persons listed in the announcement and you should call one of them to show an interest. If you ask good and relevant questions in the call there is a chance that they will remember you when they receive your application.

Before calling the recruiters you could check your network to see if you can find someone who works or has worked for the same employer. It is often very useful to talk to them to get as much inside information as possible. They can tell you about their own experience and perhaps give you some information and tips. Examples of information can be how the employer conducts their interviews; what the company strategy is, what their challenges are, what it is like to work there, important success factors for the position, and why the position became vacant.

Your questions should be planned and rehearsed in advance, so that you sound coherent and professional. I would recommend that you rehearse aloud, and in front of another person if possible, so you can hear how it sounds and make adjustments. When you feel that you are well prepared you will also be less nervous about calling.

Rehearsing is particularly important if you plan to speak Norwegian and you are apprehensive about speaking Norwegian on the phone. If so, I would recommend that you consider just introducing yourself in Norwegian, and then asking if you can switch to English when you feel that speaking Norwegian will make you sound less professional.

You can also call to ask if you can apply for the job, even if you do not speak Norwegian or if your Norwegian is not fluent. In such a case it would be best to add that you are attending a language course.

It is also acceptable to call the contact person to check if you have enough experience or relevant background for the job. You will find some examples of what I consider as good and bad questions for this phone call in chapter 3.1.

However, if you call just to engage in small talk without having any relevant questions, they may feel you are just wasting their time, which would probably work against you. You should also avoid asking questions that can be easily answered with a bit of research on the internet.

Often the first person listed in the announcement is the department leader and the second person is from HR (Human Resources or Personnel Department). I would recommend that you try to contact the department leader if possible. Show an interest in the company and position, and plan some good questions. Be prepared to make several attempts before you get hold of the contact person, and remember to ask if he or she has a few minutes in the beginning of the conversation.

Practice makes perfect: The first call you make will be the hardest, but later you will learn from your mistakes and be able to adjust your technique.

The only goal you can't accomplish is the one that you don't go after!

Vilis Ozols

2 MAKING THE APPLICATION DOCUMENTS

An application for a job in Norway consists of the following

1. Application/cover letter
2. CV
3. Attachments ((certificates, testimonials, list of publications)

This chapter will take you through the content of the application letter and CV. We will then look at some examples in chapter 3.

> It is very important that you adapt the application letter and CV for each employer and job you apply for

If you think that 'one size fits all' applications will give you the same results, you are wrong. Remember that you are competing with a lot of other candidates , and the final touch in making your application and CV fit the employer's specific requirements, may be what it takes to be called for the interview. Ref. the checklist in chapter 1.1.

Try to find out as much as possible about the employer and position by checking on the internet and using your own network., including social media. You should assume that the employers will receive a lot of applications from job-seekers. It is therefore important that your documents have a good layout, and that the content will catch the interest of the recruiters.

I would recommend that you start the process early by writing your job application letter and CV at least several days before the deadline for applying. This will give you time to let the content sink in and mature in your head for a few days. You can then read through it again with fresh eyes and adjust accordingly. This approach will probably improve the content significantly and will make it more interesting and relevant for the employer.

You should also read your application letter aloud to listen to how it sounds, in order to discover if there is anything that does not sound right.

Language

Whether your application letter and CV should be in Norwegian or English depends on your level of Norwegian. If your Norwegian is very basic then your documents should be in English. If your level is intermediate, you could try writing your application letter in Norwegian, however it would be advisable to let a Norwegian person proofread it. Your CV could be in English or Norwegian. If you claim that your Norwegian is fluent then your application letter and CV should be in Norwegian.

Make sure you use a spell-checker and that you have consistent spelling in the application letter and CV. Pay attention to how they write the company name and write it in exactly the same way.

Why is the spelling so important? Well, sometimes it is hard to make the final selection of the shortlisted candidates. It happened to me several times. If I had two candidates with an 'equal score' (the same skill sets etc.), then I would look for errors or typos in their documents as the last criteria for selection. If I found error(s) in such a formal and important document as a job application and/or CV, then I would think that this person was not very focused on quality, and I would choose the other candidate.

At this point you should bear in mind that your goal is to be called for an interview – pretending that your Norwegian is better than it really is will therefore be revealed in the interview.

2.1 Writing the application letter

The application letter is what some people call a cover letter. I will call it an application letter because it is usually called *søknadsbrev* in Norwegian, which means the same. This letter should **showcase what you can contribute with in this particular job**. It should be to the point and preferably only one page. If you find that it is just a bit more than one page, then you could try changing the format so that it will fit onto one.

A job application is a formal letter. If you write it in Norwegian, it should not have a salutation in the beginning. Norwegian letters do not have a salutation such as 'Dear Sir/Madam' or 'Dear Mr Hansen'. If you write your application letter in English you could either use a salutation or just leave it out since Norwegians are not used to salutations in letters, and they are not used to being addressed by their last name either. Chapter 3 will show you some typical examples of application letters in English and Norwegian.

As mentioned in the checklist in chapter 1.1: before writing the application you should do some self-reflection, and possibly also discuss how you are perceived by your friends, family and people you have worked with. It may be useful to analyse yourself systematically with these three categories:

- **Skills / what you are good at**
  It is a good idea to make a list of the skills you have, such as: analysing, organizing, teaching, learning new skills, motivating others, leading, working with numbers, convincing others, negotiating, written and oral skills, communicating, programming, project management, etc. Many of these may be transferred between different types of jobs.

- **Interests and hobbies**
  It is also useful to reflect upon your interests and hobbies , such as: reading, programming, politics, psychology, travel, photography, education, communication, equality, nature, sports, etc.

- **Other factors**
  You should also reflect upon such things as the minimum salary you are willing to accept, how much time you are willing to spend

travelling to work, or how much business travelling you can accept. Does the company have a 'green footprint' or make environmental friendly products?

An ideal position for you would be one that fits into key areas in all three categories above. If you feel you are applying for such a position, it is important that you convey strong motivation in your application letter.

For each of you skills, interests and other factors, you should think how you could elaborate on them in an interview situation, by using examples or telling short stories of how they might be useful in your new job and/or were useful in your previous job.

> Your goal at this stage should be getting invited for an interview

Why you are applying – motivation

The main purpose of the application letter is to explain why you are applying, and how the tasks of this particular position, as well as working for this company in general, will motivate you. In that sense, you can therefore think of it as a motivational letter.

If you called the contact person and felt that the call went well, then you should refer to it in your letter.

Many employers have little time to study the documents of each applicant. I would therefore recommend having a strong opening where the motivation clearly comes across. Such an opening should catch the interest of the employer so that they will want to continue reading. It may also be a bit personal. It could be something like this:

- With my master's degree in architecture and design, and my strong interest for sustainable architecture, I am really motivated to work in a job like this and to contribute to more environmentally friendly building techniques.

- My motivation for applying for the position as a teacher is linked to my interests. I just love to be with children and am really passionate about adopting teaching methods that will stimulate them.

- I would like to work within fisheries because I have always been interested in marine life and fishing, and really enjoy being outdoors. I believe this position would be my dream job, as I would be able to combine all of these important factors.

If you are applying from abroad, you could also consider writing why you want to move to Norway.

Address the requirements

Make sure you read the job advertisement carefully to ensure that you respond to what they are asking for. I would advise you to use a text marker on the advertisement and mark all the requirements or adjectives in the text.

Each application letter should focus on your skills and personal qualities that are relevant for this particular position and employer. Try as much as you can to match or mirror your own skills and qualifications with what they are asking for. You could either use the words you highlighted with a marker pen or you could describe the qualities in slightly different ways, along with short examples that would highlight the skills.

Be honest and describe the qualifications you have without lying about those that you lack. If they ask for a skill or personal quality that you do not have, I suggest you simply refrain from mentioning it. You should, however, be prepared to be asked about this in the interview.

Your application letter should therefore demonstrate your motivation for the job, and match the requirements in the announcement as much as possible. This is your chance to convince the employer that you are genuinely motivated as well as being suitably qualified for the position. As such, you should bear in mind that you are in effect 'selling yourself' here.

Your application letter should not simply be another version of your CV where you mostly repeat everything. In this letter, you need to emphasise why you are motivated for the job, and extract the essence from the CV that demonstrates this. If you repeat the less relevant parts from your CV in your application letter, it will be less focused, and the employers may feel that you are wasting their time by making them read the same information in two different documents.

It is also important, and the expectation, that you in the last part of the application letter write a paragraph yourself as a person. If you omit this part, you may be perceived as nerdy, or a person without any interests in life besides your own career. The employer may then be unsure as to whether you will be a good match with their existing team and to what degree you will contribute to a good working environment. Norwegian employers usually place an emphasis on this issue (ref. Chapter 5.1).

Selling yourself at the right level

Norwegians are brought up to be quite modest and they easily take a dislike and/or become suspicious of people whom they perceive as loud and bragging. Boasting about your own achievements is not part of the culture in Norway, not even in job applications.

When you write your application letter, it is important to sell yourself on the right level. By overselling, you will cause suspicion and dislike. You should also bear '*Janteloven*' in mind, which will be covered next.

In Norway, it may be difficult to find the right way of convincing a future employer that you, with your competence and your personal qualities, are a good fit for the job. It is best to promote your own achievements in a more subtle and indirect way.

In order to address their requirements as much as you can, you may use statements like:

- I like/enjoy
- I am very interested in
- I have a passion for
- I get (very) good feedback
- Other people say …

In the application letter you can sell yourself with phrases like:
- I think I am a good candidate because ...
- I will be very motivated in this position because ...
- I am very interested in this position because ...
- I think this could be the dream job for me because ...
- I believe I could contribute to the success of .... by ....

The above statements are more indirect ways of selling your competence, which sounds better and less bragging than saying outright that you are the best.

In Norway you should not oversell yourself, tell lies or exaggerate. If, however, you use the last two examples above, then you should think for a moment about what your references might say about you. If they might say something contradictory to what you have written, then the employer will become suspicious.

You will find some more tips related to this in chapter 4.3. For examples of how NOT to sell yourself, please read chapter 3.6.

Janteloven (Law of Jante)

At some point when dealing with Scandinavians you will hear about *Janteloven*, which can be considered as the suppressive side of the egalitarian culture. *Janteloven* was written by the Danish author Aksel Sandemose. It consists of ten rules which are variations of the theme: "You are not to think that you are special, or better than us".

The "law" describes the need for conformity amongst Scandinavians, and how you should not stand out too much by boasting about your own accomplishments. *Janteloven* can be seen as a good thing in some cases, such as not making losers of the masses by idolising the winners among children. In competitions for children in Norway, all participants usually receive a medal. However, the cultural urge to conform can cause a loss of self-esteem and confidence, and confine those with talents.

If you display an above- average amount of success or wealth, or visibly work much harder than your colleagues, then it may be frowned upon by Scandinavians. In Norway, the admiration of successful people that you may find in other cultures, is often associated with jealousy and dislike. There is also the perception of excessive success and wealth as being a bit vulgar.

The exception from this is winter sports in Norway, but that is another story.

It may therefore be harder to be successful in Norway, and those with success should tone it down and not brag about it, or put it too much on display. Others can brag about you, but boasting about your own wealth and achievements is considered bad taste.

The ten rules of *Janteloven*:
1. You're not to think *you* are anything special.
2. You're not to think *you* are as good as *we* are.
3. You're not to think *you* are smarter than *we* are.
4. You're not to convince yourself that *you* are better than *we* are.
5. You're not to think *you* know more than *we* do.
6. You're not to think *you* are more important than *we* are.
7. You're not to think *you* are good at anything.
8. You're not to laugh at *us*.
9. You're not to think anyone cares about you.
10. You're not to think *you* can teach *us* anything.

Janteloven

FB = Facebook

2.2 Writing the CV

CV is an abbreviation of the Latin term 'Curriculum Vitae', and is a resume of your education, career and personal qualities. The purpose of the CV is to give employers an overview in a way that will make them interested to invite you for a job interview. The term 'Resume' is also used by English speakers, but in Norway we mostly call it 'CV'.

The CV should be clear, concise, structured, easy to read, and relevant to the job you are applying for. It should be 1–3 pages, and can have attachments such as publications etc. Norwegian CVs are always in chronological order with your latest education and work experience at the top. There are some sample CVs included in chapter 3.3.

It is important that your CV does not have any time-gaps. Time-gaps may cause suspicion and speculation about what you are trying to hide from them. So if you spent time at home with your children you should list it in your CV. If went travelling around the world, mention it.

It is not enough just to adapt your application letter, as it is important also to adapt your CV each time. The CV should have more information about jobs and tasks that are relevant to the specific job for which you are applying. Usually your last job will be the most relevant, in which case you should write more about this position than for earlier ones. But if one or more of your previous jobs are more relevant to a particular position, (for example because you carried out identical or similar tasks to the ones requested in the job advert), then you must make sure that this is described properly in the CV that you are submitting.

An excellent CV is relevant for the recipient, and it is therefore important to prioritise the content. If it will not make any time-gaps in your working or educational history, you could consider omitting, adjusting or merging experience or education which is less relevant, to the job you are applying for, or if it took place a long time ago. If you are afraid that you may be overqualified for the position, you could also consider toning down some of your education or experience, but only if you are able to do it without creating any time-gaps in your CV.

If you have been unemployed for some time and have done nothing worth mentioning in your CV, it will not impress an employer. Instead of being idle it is much better to start some study (e.g. learn Norwegian), some voluntary work, or get a temporary job. Having done voluntary work looks good in a CV because it shows that you are a person who is willing to take responsibility for more than just yourself and your close family. It also looks good to have a temporary job until you get a permanent position, even if it is a low paid/status job. It shows that you are willing to work, which most employers value.

The CV should be what I call the 'Norwegian style', which is built up on the elements listed here:

Personal information header

This section should be on the top of the first or each page, with your contact information, birth date and marital status (including how many children you have and their age). It is common in Norway to write the marital status. Most employers are very accommodating towards employees with children and will not use this against you. In Norway, men also take time off from work for their parental leave, and this fact makes it less of a 'disadvantage' to be a young woman/mother in the job market.

Many people ask me if the CV should have a picture or not, and it depends on several factors. First of all, pictures are not common in academia and rarely used in the public/governmental sector.

CVs in the private industry often have photos, especially in positions with a lot of customer interaction, such as sales representative, consultant, etc.

If you decide to have a picture, then it should be neutral with a white background, and you should wear an outfit that you would wear for an interview. No sunglasses, caps, hats or similar! Avoid falling into the trap of choosing a photo of yourself doing a sports activity, on the beach or similar, as this can make you look rather unprofessional.

2. Making the application documents

Research (9) shows that for a woman it is best not to appear too glamorous in the picture, unless applying for a modelling job or similar. Some employers may find that good looks take some focus away from work, so you should tone down any good looks you might have. This means that makeup should be minimal, and long hair should be pulled back or in a ponytail so that it is not the focus of the picture. Needless to say, there should be no cleavage showing in the picture either.

Any display of religious symbols may reduce your chances of being invited to an interview with some employers. Norway is a secular society, and many employers expect their staff not to put their religious beliefs on display. There have been several debates about this in recent years – the one with the most media coverage was whether hijab should be allowed in the Norwegian Police.

The outcome was that hijab is not allowed with the police uniform because police officers are supposed to be neutral and not display any religious beliefs when they are on duty. This may however be changed over time.

Research (10) also shows that job-seekers with non-Norwegian names or looks have less chance of being invited for job interviews. I know of non-Norwegians who have used the family name of their Norwegian spouse when applying for jobs in Norway, with good results. The same research also shows that the small and medium sized companies are more skeptical towards foreign candidates than large companies, who usually have several non-Norwegians in their staff already.

From summer 2019 the government will initiate a trial project where the name of the applicant for positions in the public/governmental sector will be made anonymous. This is being done in an effort to make it easier for foreign job-seekers to get work in Norway. This project is estimated to last for approximately 18 months.

If you send your CV from outside of Norway, you should add your nationality under the personal information header. You should also remember to include your country's prefix with your telephone number.

Key qualifications

This is perhaps the most important section of your CV. Many employers have very little time to spend reading each CV, perhaps only spending a few seconds. Your key qualifications will be a bit like a management summary of your CV – the employer will probably start by reading this part to quickly decide if they should continue reading.

This section should be 3-10 lines or bullet points with a summary of your competence, experience, skills and personal qualities. This section should be adapted to each position you are applying for, and the list should be arranged in the order of relevance for this particular job. When working to define your key qualifications, it is important that you make an effort to see yourself in a holistic light. As previously mentioned, you should look for any skills and/or talents that may be useful in the position you are applying for.

Education incl. NOKUT recognition

Your education should be listed in chronological order with the newest at the top. If you have completed higher education at Bachelors, Masters and/or PhD degree level, then you can leave out secondary school from the list.

Job experience

Your job experience should also be listed in chronological order with the newest at the top. Each job should have a short description (1–4 lines). If you have a lot of job experience you should write more about the most recent and/or relevant jobs, and less about the older and/or less relevant jobs, to avoid the CV exceeding more than 3 pages.

You should also add the following information
- Relevant courses
- Languages
- Voluntary work and similar
- Other (e.g. driving license)
- Interests/hobbies

You can also include how long you have spent in Norway, if any.

References

The final section of your CV should be your references. It is very important to have some references when applying for a job in Norway. It is equally important that you ask them if they are willing to be your reference before you include their contact information in your CV.

If you need time to find and talk to your references, you can buy yourself more time by writing the sentence 'References will be provided upon request' in the reference section. This may also free up valuable space in the CV for other information without it growing too long.

You should expect your references to be checked and that they will give your future employer honest feedback about you. Bear in mind what they might say about you when you try to sell yourself in your job application, and more importantly the interview. If you write or say something that contradicts what your references will say then you greatly reduce your chances of getting the job.

You should strive to have some references in Norway, as Norwegian employers will be less inclined to contact references abroad. The larger geographical/cultural distance the less value there will be in your references.

If you use references outside Norway you should specify which language they speak in brackets next to their name.

Finding references in Norway for your first job can be difficult. If you have done any voluntary work, you could ask someone in the organisation you worked for to be your reference. If you are a student you could ask your tutor or supervisor. You should study the section 'The value of voluntary work' later in this chapter and chapter 6 for more tips.

Web recruitment systems

Some employers use an online recruitment system because it is more convenient for them, automating part of the handling of applications. However, online systems are more work for you, because you have to fill in each field of their forms instead of just customising and submitting your application letter and CV. But the employers define the rules, so doing the boring and time-consuming task of filling in field by field cannot be avoided.

Even for online systems, it is always best to have a proper, spell-checked application letter and CV in electronic format such as Word or similar that you can copy and paste from. Writing directly into the online system could be difficult and may give some unwanted results. I therefore advise that you customise your own application letter and CV before copying and pasting it into the different fields of the web recruitment system.

It is important that you always submit an application letter, even when using web recruitment systems. Some employers will not consider applicants who have not bothered to submit an application letter. These candidates are not considered committed enough.

Portablecv.org is an organisation that can help you by exporting your CV from one online system to another. It will then generate a file on your computer that can be imported into other web recruitment portals. If the web recruitment system supports this, there will be a button called *'portableCV eksport'* for this export.

The value of voluntary work

As mentioned earlier, voluntary work for a non-Governmental organisation (NGO) has a high value in Norway. It looks impressive on the CV, as it shows that you are a person who is willing to take responsibility for others and help those who have not been as fortunate in life as yourself. It is also a good way of getting your first Norwegian reference.

Examples of NGOs with voluntary work are the Red Cross, *Kirkens bymisjon,* (Church Mission helping people in poverty or difficult situations), *or Natteravnene (Night Ravens,* patrolling the streets at night, talking to people and helping those who need it). **Frivillig.no** (12) is a portal where you can look up this kind of work. Voluntary work done outside Norway also has a high value and should be included in the CV too.

2.3 Testimonials

Testimonial is called *attest* in Norwegian and is a document issued by previous employers as proof that you have worked there. Copies of your testimonials are submitted to the prospective employer together with copies of your certificates. You can, by law, demand to get a testimonial from your employer when you leave a job. A standard testimonial only states your name, your birthdate, your position and when you worked there.

If they were satisfied with your work, employers will often write something more than this, but you cannot demand it. You should always ask for a testimonial before you leave an employer or organisation. You should also be able to get testimonials for part-time and voluntary work.

Some employers may ask you to draft your own testimonial. Do not be shocked if this happens – this is actually a huge advantage for you. Remember there is power in the pen, and nobody knows better than you what tasks you have carried out or been responsible for.

I have enclosed an example of a good testimonial in chapter 3.4 so that you can see what it looks like and get some ideas. You should write down all the tasks you have carried out and especially make sure to mention what your responsibilities were.

The last part in the sample testimonial in chapter 3.4 is about personal qualities, and you should not add this part. If you are lucky and the employer is satisfied with you, something like this will be added by them.

There is also a reference to a testimonial template (11) in the reference section of this book.

Successful people are always looking for opportunities to help others. Unsuccessful people are always asking, "What's in it for me?"

Brian Tracy

3 EXAMPLES

3.1 Questions for the phone call

Here are some examples of questions for the phone call with the contact person in the announcement:

Good questions

- You are asking for someone with experience. I have recently finished my Masters, and have had some part-time jobs working in shops until now. I am, however, very motivated for this job and think I have the right background. Do you think I should apply?

- You are asking for international experience. Whilst I do not have international work experience, I am from Iran and have studied in the UK and have travelled a lot. Would you consider this kind of experience relevant?

- Which of the tasks in the announcement are the most important and which would you consider less important?

- I feel that I would be a good candidate for the job, but I still have six months left of my maternity leave. Would it still be relevant for me to apply?

- I see that this position entails handling deviations and complaints. How often do they happen, and for what reasons?

- When do you expect to be ready to start the interview process?

- When is the expected start-date for this position?
  (Only if it is not mentioned in the announcement).

Bad or inappropriate questions

- What does your company do and what are the tasks of this job?
  This information can easily be found on the internet and in the job announcement.

- Can I send you my CV for you to have a look at to see if I should apply?
  This would give them extra work in a busy recruitment process, and it shows that you have not given this any thought.

- How much would you pay someone with 3 years' experience?
  This gives the impression that money is the main motivation for you, and they would probably want someone who is motivated by other factors, such as the tasks, work environment, company profile etc.

- How many people have applied for this job?
  They may feel this is none of your business.

- Do you have a friend who will fill this position, or is this position really vacant?
  The best candidate will get the position, and filling a position with a friend should not happen in Norway. There is, however, another situation which may occur, and this is explained in the next chapter.

3.2 Temporary position becoming permanent

Sometimes temporary positions are made permanent because of an increased budget, grants or similar. When this happens, there is already someone working in this position. If this person is doing a good job and has already proven what he or she are good for, then they are likely to get the job.

In the public/governmental sector, including academia, the rules are that all vacancies are required to be announced in the market. So even if they already have a good candidate for the job, the normal recruitment process has to be followed. It will be very hard for you to compete with somebody who is already in this positon, if he or she is doing a good job. However, if your qualifications are superior to the person who is temporary in that role, you should get the job.

In order for you to find out if this is the case for the job you want to apply for, you could ask during the phone call with the interviewer:

- Is this position newly created?

If the position is not new, you could then ask a follow up question:

- Has the person who previously had this position left or retired?

This will be a way of finding out if the position is vacant because somebody left, or if is a temporary one which is being made permanent. If the latter happens to be the case, you could ask:

- Is it likely that the person who is working there now will apply for this position?

If they tell you that they have a candidate who is already working in that particular position, you can still apply, but you should be aware that you will probably only be shortlisted if your qualifications are far superior to the present candidate.

In chapter 6.1 I mention how you could position yourself to be the candidate in the temporary position which may become permanent later.

3.3 Application letter samples

Below you will find some sample application letters in English and Norwegian.

John Smith
Kaosveien 7
0999 Oslo   13th November 2017

ABC
Storgata 10
0991 Oslo

Application for the position of Building Technology Advisor

With reference to the advertisement on Finn.no and the pleasant phone call on 6 November with Nils Nilsen, I wish to apply for the vacant position of Building Technology Advisor.

I am very personally concerned about climate change, and hope to find a position where I will be able to contribute to reversing its negative effects. Since this job will give me the opportunity to work with energy efficiency and environmental issues related to building, I believe this could be the dream job for me.

I graduated in autumn 2012 from the University of Environment and Biological Sciences (UMB) with a degree in civil engineering specializing in 'Civil Engineering and Architecture'. My thesis was a research-based depiction of strength properties of clay plaster and was submitted in August this year. I am 27 years old and originally from England.

I understand from the phone conversation with Nils Nilsen that this position will entail consulting and client relations, as well as sizing and calculations related to ABC's products. At UMB I had the opportunity to work with these topics and I have extensive industry contacts in connection with my thesis. Since I enjoyed this combination, I think the position would suit me perfectly.

I have a broad background in statics and building physics from the university. I have studied several in-depth subjects, where one of them involved the simulation of heat using various computer programs. I have also been involved in developing civil engineering solutions to meet environmental requirements. As chairman of the association for sustainable housing (NJH), I have also worked a great deal with public relations and communication. This knowledge and experience could therefore be useful at ABC.

I am motivated by being able to make positive contributions as part of a team, and I think that I will really enjoy working in a small department of a large company such as ABC.

I look forward to hearing from you and am hoping for a positive response to this application.

Yours faithfully,

John Smith

This application has the following attachments:
- *CV*
- *Contact information of reference persons*

John Smith
Kaosveien 7
0999 Oslo   13. november 2017

ABC
Storgata 10
0991 Oslo

Søknad på stilling som byggteknisk rådgiver

Jeg viser til annonse på Finn.no og takker for hyggelig telefonsamtale 6. november med Nils Nilsen. Etter avtale ønsker jeg med dette å søke stillingen som byggteknisk rådgiver.

Jeg er personlig veldig bekymret over klimaendringene, og jeg håper å finne en stilling hvor jeg kan være med å bidra til å reversere den negative utviklingen. Siden denne jobben vil gi meg mulighet til å arbeide med energieffektive løsninger og miljøvennlige løsninger innen byggfag, tenker jeg at dette kan være drømmejobben min.

Jeg er nyutdannet høsten 2012 fra Universitetet for Miljø og Biovitenskap med en sivilingeniørgrad innen studieretningen 'Byggeteknikk og arkitektur'. Masteroppgaven min var en forskningsbasert skildring av fasthetsegenskaper i leirpuss og ble levert inn i august i år. Jeg er 27 år og kommer opprinnelig fra England.

Slik jeg forstod stillingen på telefon med Nils Nilsen, vil den inneha både rådgiving og kundekontakt, samt dimensjonering og beregninger knyttet til ABC sine produkter. På UMB har jeg fått anledning til å arbeide med faglige problemstillinger og jeg har fått utstrakt bransjekontakt i forbindelse med min masteroppgave. Denne kombinasjonen har jeg likt godt, og med bakgrunn i en slik erfaring tror jeg denne stillingen vil passe meg ypperlig.

På universitet har jeg foruten bred bakgrunn innen statikk og bygningsfysikk, gjennomført flere frivillige fordypningsfag hvor ett av dem omhandlet simulering av varmetap ved hjelp av ulike data-program. Gjennom en praksisperiode ved et arkitektkontor i London var jeg med på å utvikle byggetekniske løsninger for å møte miljøsertifiseringskrav. Som leder for en interesseforening for bærekraftig husbygging (NJH), har jeg også jobbet en god del med informasjonsarbeid og henvendelser fra interesserte. Dette er kunnskap og erfaring som ser ut til å være nyttig hos ABC.

Jeg motiveres av å kunne bidra positivt som en del av et lag og tror at jeg vil trives svært godt med å jobbe i en liten avdeling av et så stort selskap som ABC. Å jobbe med energieffektivisering og miljøspørsmål knyttet til bygg, opplever jeg personlig som svært meningsfylt og dette vil være en ekstra motivasjonsfaktor for meg i det daglige arbeidet.

Jeg ser fram til å høre fra dere og håper på en positiv behandling av søknaden!

Med vennlig hilsen

John Smith

Denne søknaden har følgende vedlegg:
- *CV*
- *Kontaktinformasjon til referansepersoner*

Gonzalo Garcia
Snarveien 16
5000 BERGEN
Tel.: . 999 33 888

30th January 2018

WILCO AS
Kolbotnveien 55
0112 OSLO

APPLICATION FOR THE VACANT 'CONSTRUCTION MANAGER' POSITION

With reference to my telephone conversation with Geir Monsen yesterday and the advertisement in TU # 1/18, I would like to apply for the above.

I think that my master's degree from the construction line at Madrid College of Engineering (1995) as well as my experience as a project engineer in XYZ ASA, in combination with my organising skills and solution oriented mind-set would make me a very good candidate for this position.

I am 37 years old and from Spain. I currently work as a project engineer in XYZ ASA, a company I have worked for since August 2007. Whilst at XYZ I have been involved in the construction of commercial and office buildings, storage facilities, as well as a residential and rehabilitation centre with a hospital. I am responsible for the planning and monitoring of all types of construction. Furthermore, I have experience with case calculation and conservation management.

Before starting at XYZ, I worked for six months in office building projects in Arna municipality, where I carried out inspections (height, operation and inspections on completion) as well as other public services and trouble-shooting in connection with building projects. It required a good understanding of the Planning and Building Act.

As a person I am stable, loyal and cooperative. I have a positive outlook and good oral and written skills. I like to be solution-oriented and efficient, which I think my references (names to be supplied on request) will confirm.

I kindly request confidential treatment of this application until I have informed my current employer that I am seeking another job. I am looking forward to your reply to this application!

Yours faithfully,

Gonzalo Garcia

Gonzalo Garcia
Snarveien 16
5000 BERGEN   30. januar 2018
Tlf. 999 33 888

WILCO AS
Kolbotnveien 55
0112 OSLO

SØKNAD PÅ LEDIG STILLING SOM BYGGELEDER/PROSJEKTLEDER

Jeg viser til telefonsamtale med Geir Monsen i går samt annonse i TU nr. 2/08, og jeg ønsker herved å søke denne stillingen.

Jeg tror at min master innen bygg- og anleggslinjen ved Madrid College of Engineering (1995), min erfaring som prosjektingeniør i XYZ ASA i kombinasjon med mine organisatoriske ferdigheter og løsningsorienterte innstilling vil være en svært god kandidat for denne stillingen.

Jeg er 37 år gammel og fra Spania. Jeg arbeider i dag som prosjektingeniør hos XYZ ASA, et selskap jeg har jobbet for siden august 2012. I XYZ har jeg vært med på bygging av næringsbygg/ kontorbygg, lagerhall, samt et bo- og rehabiliteringssenter med sykehus. Jeg har hatt ansvar for planlegging og oppfølging av alle typer byggetekniske fag. Videre har jeg erfaring med prosjektkalkulasjon og verneledelse.

Før jeg begynte i XYZ jobbet jeg et halvt år på byggesakskontoret i Arna kommune, der jeg drev med befaringer (høyde-, bruks- og ferdigbefaring) og annen type service/problemløsing ovenfor publikum i forbindelse med byggesaker. Stillingen krevde god innsikt i plan- og bygningsloven.

Som person er jeg stabil, lojal og samarbeidsvillig. Jeg har en positiv innstilling og god muntlig og skriftlig formuleringsevne. Samtidig liker jeg å være handlingsorientert og å finne gode løsninger, noe jeg tror mine referanser (navn oppgis på forespørsel) vil bekrefte.

Jeg må be om konfidensiell behandling av søknaden overfor nåværende arbeidsgiver. Jeg ser med stor forventning frem til svar på denne søknaden!

Med vennlig hilsen

Gonzalo Garcia

Pawel Garvan
Kaosveien 13
1200 OSLO   10th March 2019
Tlf. 999 99 999
paw.garvan@gmail.com

ABC
Blåsbortveien 1
1000 OSLO

Application for the position as a carpenter

With reference to the advertisement on Finn.no and my recent telephone conversation with Nils Nilsen, I hereby apply for the advertised position as a carpenter.

I am a 24-year-old man from Poland who has been in Norway for three years. I enjoy very much working with carpentry. I have always liked working with my hands, especially natural materials, such as wood and stone.

I have recently completed a 3 month internship in Norway where I received an introduction to how the carpentry profession is practiced in Norway. In Poland, I was trained by my grandfather who was a carpenter. He taught me to work hard, and together we carried out different types of repairs for people in the neighborhood.

Although the carpentry profession can be quite busy, I am able to handle stress quite well. I work quickly and like it when many things happen around me. I also enjoy working with other people and in a team.

I hope I will be considered for a position in you company, and look forward to hearing from you.

Kind regards,

Pawel Garvan

Pawel Garvan
Kaosveien 13
1200 OSLO
Tlf. 999 99 999
paw.garvan@gmail.com

10. mars 2019

ABC
Blåsbortveien 1
1000 OSLO

Søknad på stilling som tømrer

Jeg viser til annonse på Finn.no, samt telefonsamtale med Nils Nilsen og søker herved den utlyste stillingen som tømrer.

Jeg er 24 år gammel mann fra Polen som har vært i Norge i tre år, og som er svært motivert for å jobbe innenfor tømrerfaget. Jeg har alltid likt å jobbe med hendene og trives svært godt med å jobbe med levende materialer som tre og stein.

Jeg har nylig avsluttet en 3 måneders praksisperiode i Norge, hvor jeg fikk en innføring i hvordan tømrerfaget utøves. I Polen fikk jeg opplæring av min bestefar som var tømrer. Han lærte meg å jobbe hardt, og sammen påtok vi oss forskjellige typer snekkeroppgaver for folk i nabolaget.

Selv om tømreryrket kan være ganske hektisk, mener jeg at jeg takler stress ganske bra. Jeg jobber raskt og liker at det skjer ting rundt meg. Jeg trives også godt med å samarbeide med andre personer og føle at jeg jobber i et lag.

Jeg håper jeg vil komme i betraktning til en jobb hos dere og ser fram til å høre fra dere.

Med vennlig hilsen

Pawel Garvan

Yana Hussami
Kaosveien 13
1200 OSLO
Tlf. 999 99 999
yana.hussami@gmail.com

10th March 2019

ABC
Blåsbortveien 1
1000 OSLO

Application for the position as shop assistant

I refer to the advertisement on Finn.no and the phone call with Line Jensen. I would like to apply for the advertised position as a shop assistant.

I am a 29 year old woman from Syria who has lived in Norway for three years. I consider ABC as an interesting workplace for me, because I have heard a lot of positive things about your shop.

I have some experience from shop work where I have packed goods, refilled the stock and working with the cash register. I especially liked working as a checkout operator, because I had the chance to meet many nice people, and at the same time I could practice speaking Norwegian.

As a person I am punctual, responsible and flexible. Those who know me will describe me as a good-tempered person who is not afraid of hard work.

I would like to contribute to giving ABC's customers as good service as possible. I hope for a positive treatment of this application and look forward to hearing from you.

Yours faithfully,

Yana Hussami

3. Examples

Yana Hussami
Kaosveien 13
1200 OSLO   10. mars 2019
Tlf. 999 99 999
yana.hussami@gmail.com

ABC
Blåsbortveien 1
1000 OSLO

Søknad på stilling som butikkmedarbeider

Jeg viser til annonse på Finn.no og telefonsamtale med Line Jensen. Jeg vil gjerne søke på den utlyste stillingen som butikkmedarbeider.

Jeg er en 29 år gammel kvinne fra Syria som har bodd i Norge i tre år. Grunnen til at jeg søker, er at jeg ser på ABC som en interessant arbeidsplass fordi jeg har hørt mye positivt om dere.

Jeg har noe erfaring fra butikkarbeid hvor jeg har pakket ut varer, fylt i hyller og sittet i kassen. Jeg likte spesielt godt kassearbeidet fordi jeg fikk treffe mange hyggelige mennesker, samtidig som det var god øvelse i å snakke norsk.

Som person er jeg punktlig, ansvarsbevisst og fleksibel. De som kjenner meg vil beskrive meg som en person med godt humør som ikke er redd for å ta i et tak.

Jeg ønsker å bidra til at ABC sine kunder skal få så god service som mulig. Jeg håper på en positiv behandling av denne søknaden og ser fram til å høre fra dere.

Med vennlig hilsen

Yana Hussami

Bilan Amburo
Kaosveien 13
1200 OSLO   10th March 2019
Tlf. 999 99 999
b-amburo@gmail.com

ABC
Blåsbortveien 1
1000 OSLO

Application for the position as cleaner

I refer to the advertisement on NAV.no and telephone conversation with Kari Nilsen and hereby apply for the vacant position as a cleaner.

I am a 32 year old woman from Somalia. I think the part-time position at ABC would be perfect for me because it can be combined with having small children and studying Norwegian.

I have some experience from cleaning work, where I have worked with daily and periodic cleaning at a school. I have a class B driving license.

As a person I am punctual, responsible and structured. Those who know me will describe me as a hard-working person with an eye for detail.

 I feel I have what it takes to do a good job for you and look forward to hearing from you.

Yours faithfully,

Bilan Amburo

Bilan Amburo
Kaosveien 13
1200 OSLO   10. mars 2019
Tlf. 999 99 999
b-amburo@gmail.com

ABC
Blåsbortveien 1
1000 OSLO

Søknad på stilling som renholder

Jeg viser til annonse på NAV.no og telefonsamtale med Kari Nilsen og søker herved den utlyste stillingen som renholder.

Jeg er en 32 år gammel kvinne fra Somalia. Jeg tror deltidsstillingen hos ABC er ideell for meg fordi den kan kombineres med å være småbarnsmor og ha norskstudier ved siden av.

Jeg har noe erfaring fra renholdsarbeid, hvor jeg har arbeidet med daglig og periodisk renhold på en skole. Jeg har førerkort klasse B.

Som person er jeg punktlig, ansvarsbevisst og strukturert. De som kjenner meg vil beskrive meg som en hardtarbeidende person med øye for detaljer.

Jeg føler jeg har de nødvendige forutsetningene for å gjøre en god jobb hos dere og ser fram til å høre fra dere.

Med vennlig hilsen

Bilan Amburo

3.4 CV samples

CV – LENE HANSEN

Address	Olavs gate 29, 0354 OSLO
E-mail	lene.hansen@gmail.com
Telephone	+47 911 99 009
Birth date	15.12.1980
Marital status	Married with one child (5 years old)

KEY QUALIFICATIONS

International relations and human rights
Ability to build relationships and network in diverse environments
Experience with strategic and operational work in complex organisations
Experienced course instructor for adults and youths

EDUCATION

8/2002 – 6/2007   **University of Bergen (UiB)**
Master's degree in human rights and cultural diversity
Master's thesis: Human Rights in Post-Soviet States

8/2000 – 6/2002   **University of Oslo (UiO)**
One-year studies in social studies, humanity, culture, history and dialog-building
Russian basic and intermediate courses

8/1999 – 6/2000   **Au pair in London**
Worked and lived with a British family. Language courses

WORK EXPERIENCE

3/2012 – Today   **PR Advisor in the Peace Group**
Development and implementation of new communication strategy as well as common processes for the Norwegian organisation
Development of training programme and material. Responsible for publishing information on the website and social media
Management of communication projects related to events and campaigns
Production of newsletter in English to the international organisation and partners

1/2009 – 3/2012	**Communication Consultant in Clarity ASA** Responsible for content of the internal and external webpage This position required the constant monitoring of press coverage and external media, as well as communication with external partners, interviews, editing and some translation from English and Russian
6/2006 – 12/2008	**Financial Assistant in KEM** Accounting work, mainly posting incoming invoices Started with reception work part-time 2006–2007 Secretarial work as a summer job in 2006
5/2004 – 6/2006	**PR Assistant, Visit Norway Tourist Information** Making brochures, giving information and advice to tourists
6/2002 – 5/2004	**Red Cross** Voluntary work as a visiting friend for an old and lonely man

COURSES

1999 – 2000	Russian language study in St. Petersburg
Spring 2003	Russian language course at NKI

LANGUAGES

English	Fluent written and verbally
Russian	Very good written, fluent verbally
Norwegian	Good written and verbally

ORGANISATIONAL WORK

2001-2002	Leader of the Russian Association at UiO
2003-2006	Market responsible for the Student Union at UiO

OTHER

Interests	Listening to podcasts, reading, skiing and music

REFERENCES

To be provided upon request.

CV – Lene Hansen

Adresse	Olavs gate 29, 0354 OSLO
E-post	lene.hansen@gmail.com
Telefon	+47 911 99 009
Født	15.12.1980
Sivilstand	Gift, med ett barn (5 år)

Nøkkelkvalifikasjoner

Internasjonale relasjoner og menneskerettigheter
Evne til å bygge relasjoner og nettverk i flerkulturelle miljøer
Erfaring med strategisk og operasjonelt arbeid i komplekse organisasjoner
Erfaren kursinstruktør for voksne og barn

Utdanning

8/2002 – 6/2007 **Universitetet i Bergen (UiB)**
Master i menneskerettigheter og kulturelt mangfold
Masteroppgave: Menneskerettigheter i tidligere Sovjetstater

8/2000 – 6/2002 **Universitetet i Oslo (UiO)**
Et års studium i sosiale fag, humanitet, kultur, historie og dialogbygging
Russisk grunnfag og mellomfag

8/1999 – 6/2000 **Au pair i London**
Jobbet og bodde hos en britisk familie. Språkkurs

Arbeidserfaring

3/2012 – i dag **PR rådgiver i Fredsgruppen**
Utvikling og implementering av ny kommunikasjonsstrategi samt felles prosesser for organisasjonen. Utvikling av opplæringsprogram og –materiell. Ansvar for å publisere informasjon på hjemmeside og sosiale medial. Lede kommunikasjonsprosjekter i forbindelse med arrangementer og kampanjer. Produsere nyhetsbrev på engelsk for den internasjonale organisasjonen og samarbeidspartnere.

1/2009 – 3/2012	**Kommunikasjonskonsulent i Clarity ASA** Ansvar for innholdet på intranettet og ekstern hjemmeside Stillingen krevde overvåking av pressedekning og eksterne media, samt kommunikasjon med eksterne partnere, intervjuer, redigering og oversettelse fra russisk og engelsk
6/2006 – 12/2008	**Regnskapsassistent i KEM** Regnskapsarbeid, hovedsakelig postering av fakturaer Startet som resepsjonsmedarbeider på deltid 2006–2007 Sekretærarbeid som sommervikar i 2006
5/2004 – 6/2006	**Visit Norway turistinformasjon** Lage brosjyrer, informasjon og veiledning av turister
1/2002 – 4/2004	**Røde Kors** Frivillig arbeid som besøksvenn for en eldre og ensom mann

KURS

1999– 2000	Russisk språk studier i St. Petersburg
Våren 2003	Russisk språkkurs, NKI

SPRÅK

Engelsk	Flytende skriftlig og muntlig
Russisk	Meget godt skriftlig og flytende muntlig
Norsk	Godt skriftlig og muntlig

ORGANISASJONSARBEID

2001– 2002	Leder for den russiske forening ved UiO
2003– 2006	Markedsansvarlig for studentunionen ved UiO

ANNET

Fritidsinteresser Lytte til podcaster, lese, ski og musikk.

REFERANSER
Oppgis ved forespørsel.

Applying for jobs in Norway

JOHN SMITH

Kaosveien 7, 0999 Oslo   Tel. 99 99 99 99
john.smith@student.no
Birth date: 25th August 1985 | Marital status: married

Key Qualifications

- Construction engineering in combination with architectural skills
- Construction of energy efficient buildings
- Fatigue calculation, stress testing and reporting

Education

August 2006 – June 2011	**Master's degree** **Building techniques and architecture** Wood construction and technology Thesis: 'Effect of clay plaster'	*University of Environment and Biological Sciences (UMB)*
August 2005 – June 2006	**Basic study, natural science** Preparatory year for the engineering study	*University of Environment and Biological Sciences*
August 2001 – June 2004	**Allmennfaglig studieretning** In-depth study: 'Wooden furniture'	*Rudolf Steiner School in Bergen*

Work experience

September 2011 – today	**Bridge inspection engineer** Inspection of bridges to see if and how they need to be maintained. Fatigue calculation and reporting	*Brobyggeverket*
October 2008	**Voluntary work** Building of a traditional farmhouse in Portugal	*World Wide Organic Farms*
January 2008 – June 2008	**Kindergarten Assistant** Temporary position working 60% for a department with 25 children	*Fjell barnehage*
Sept. 2005 – January 2008	**Leader of a student choir** Member of the board, financial responsibility and responsible for the planning and implementation of a student show	*Song Choir at UMB*
June 2007 – August 2007	**Voluntary work** Building work at a school near St. Petersburg	*BRO Foundation*

Other experience

March 2005 January 2010	– **Farm worker** Shorter periods of work on farms in Germany, Spain and Portugal, to learn languages and culture	
July 2008 December 2008	– **Cultural travel** Cultural travel to seven countries in Europe with my fiancé in our self-made camping van	
Sept 2004 December 2004	– **Farm worker** Practical and diverse full-time work in a large Icelandic farm with 30 cows and 800 sheep.	*Hallhjem,* *Iceland*

Languages

English	Native	**German**	Good
Norwegian	Good		

IT competence

In general very good IT-competence, such as Microsoft Office, picture processing software, Windows and Linux

I have extensive experience of the following computer programs, having used them as part of my university courses. These count for almost 30 study credits from my curriculum

Vectorworks	(CAD)	SIMIEN	(simulation of energy)
ArchiCad	(CAD)	THERM	(simulation of frost)
Focus Construction	(FEM-analysis)	Matlab	(programming)
Focus Tender	(tender description)	Python	(programming)
WUFI	(simulation of dampness)		

Relevant courses

Driving licence: Class B   Diving certificate

References

Per Hansen, Departmental manager of Fjell barnehage
Lise Nilsen, Leader of the Song Choir at UMB
Igor Zacharchenko, Director of ABC Architects in St. Petersburg
Trond Hansen, Manager of BA group of Manpower Oslo

The contact information of these reference persons will be provided upon request.

JOHN SMITH

Kaosveien 7, 0999 Oslo   Tlf. 99 99 99 99
john.smith@student.no
Fødselsdato: 25. august 1985 | Sivilstatus: gift

Nøkkelkvalifikasjoner

- Sivilingeniør innen byggeteknikk og arkitektur
- Konstruksjon av energieffektive bygninger
- Tretthetsberegning, stresstesting og rapportering

Utdanning

August 2006 – juni 2011	**Femårig master i teknologi (sivilingeniør) Byggeteknikk og arkitektur** Trekonstruksjoner og treteknologi Oppgave: 'Skivevirking i leirepuss'	*Universitet for Miljø og Biovitenskap (UMB)*
August 2005 – juni 2006	**Grunnstudium, naturvitenskap** Forberedende år for ingeniørstudiet	*Universitet for Miljø og Biovitenskap*
August 2001 – juni 2004	**Allmennfaglig studieretning** Fordypning: 'Møbelarbeider i tre'	*Rudolf Steinerskolen i Bergen*

Arbeidserfaring

September 2011 – i dag	**Ingeniør for broinspeksjon** Inspeksjon av broer for å evaluere om og hvordan de skal vedlikeholdes. Tretthetsberegning og rapportering	*Brobyggeverket*
Oktober 2008	**Frivillig arbeid** Bygging av tradisjonelt våningshus i Portugal	*World Wide Organic Farms*
Januar 2008 – juni 2008	**Barnehageassistent** Deltidsstilling (60%) i en avdeling med 25 barn	*Fjell barnehage*
September 2005 – januar 2008	**Leder for et studentkor** Medlem av styret, økonomiansvarlig, samt ansvarlig for oppsetting av studentrevy	*Sangkoret ved UMB*
Juni 2007 – august 2007	**Frivillig arbeid** Bygging av hus på en skole ved St. Petersburg	*BRO Stiftelsen*

Annen erfaring

Mars 2005 – januar 2010	**Gårdsarbeider** Kortere arbeidsopphold på gårder i Tyskland, Spania og Portugal for å lære språk og kultur	
Juli 2008 – desember 2008	**Kulturreise** Kulturreise til sju land i Europa med min kommende kone i vår selvbygde bobil	
September 2004 – desember 2004	**Gårdsarbeider** Praktisk og allsidig fulltidsengasjement på Islandsk storgård med 30 melkekyr og 800 sauer	*Hallhjem, Island*

Språk

Engelsk	Flytende	**Tysk**	Godt
Norsk	Godt		

IT-ferdigheter

Generelt svært gode IT-ferdigheter. Svært god kjennskap til Office-pakken, bildebehandlingsprogrammer, Windows og Linux

Med bakgrunn fra universitetskurs behersker jeg følgende dataverktøy. Dette utgjør nærmere 30 studiepoeng av min studieplan

Vectorworks	(CAD)	SIMIEN	(energisimulering)
ArchiCad	(CAD)	THERM	(simulering av frost)
Focus Construction	(FEM-analyse)	Matlab	(programmering)
Focus Tender	(anbudsbeskrivelse)	Python	(programmering)
WUFI	(fukt/varmesimulering)		

Relevante kurs

Førerkort: Klasse B   Dykkersertifikat

Referanser

Per Hansen, avdelingsleder i Fjellhus barnehage
Lise Nilsen, leder av sangkoret ved UMB
Igor Zacharchenko, Director of ABC Architects, St. Petersburg
Trond Hansen, Leder av BA gruppen I Manpower, Oslo

Kontaktinformasjonen til ovennevnte referansepersoner kan utleveres på forespørsel.

CV – PAWEL GARVAN

Adress	Kaosveien 13, 1200 OSLO
E-mail	paw.garvan@gmail.com
Telephone	+47 999 99 999
Birth date	12.02.1995
Marital status	Married, one child (3 years)

Work experience

9/2015-today	**Gnisten idrettslag** Voluntary work as a football coach for a boys' team, 10 – 12 years old
9/2018-12/2018	**Internship in Norwegian carpentry and work culture at Tømmermenn A/S** Attended an introductory course as a carpenter in Norway
6/2012-3/2015	**Carpenter together with my granddad in Poland** Versatile woodwork carpentry, some masonry work with rocks and concrete

Education

8/2015-today	**Speak Norsk, Oslo** Norwegian language course, level B2
8/2009-6/2012	**XYZ secondary school in Poland** Three years of secondary school

Courses

2016	Introduction to Norway for newly arrived immigrants
2017	Norwegian driving license class B (manual gears)

Languages

Polish	Native, written and oral
Norwegian	Intermediate, written and oral

Other

Interests	Football, craftsmanship and singing in a choir

References

Petter Olsen, construction leader at Tømmermenn A/S, tel. 99 99 99 99
Ove Myre, leader at Gnisten idrettslag, tel. 99 99 99 99

CV – PAWEL GARVAN

Adresse	Kaosveien 13, , 1200 OSLO
E-post	paw.garvan@gmail.com
Telefon	+47 999 99 999
Født	12.02.1995
Sivilstand	Gift, ett barn (3 år)

Arbeidserfaring

9/2015-i dag   **Gnisten idrettslag**
Frivillig arbeid som fotballtrener for et guttelag 10 – 12 år

9/2018-12/2018   **Praksiskurs i norsk arbeidsliv hos Tømmermenn A/S**
Deltatt på et 3 måneders praksisprogram med innføring tømreryrket

6/2012-3/2015   **Tømrer hos min bestefar i Polen**
Allsidig tømrerarbeid i tre, noe murarbeid med stein og betong

Utdanning

8/2015-i dag   **Speak Norsk, Oslo**
Norskkurs, nivå B2

8/2010-6/2012   **XYZ ungdomsskole i Polen**
Treårig ungdomsskole

Kurs

2016   Introduksjon for nyankomne innvandrere

2017   Norsk førerkort klasse B (manuelt gir)

Språk

Polsk   Flytende skriftlig og muntlig

Norsk   Godt skriftlig og muntlig

Annet

Fritidsinteresser   Fotball, håndverk og korsang

Referanser

Petter Olsen, anleggsleder hos Tømmermenn A/S, tlf. 99 99 99 99
Ove Myre, leder ved Gnisten idrettslag, tlf. 99 99 99 99

Applying for jobs in Norway

CV – Yana Hussami

Address	Kaosveien 13, 1200 OSLO
E-mail	yana.hussami@gmail.com
Telephone	+47 999 99 999
Birth date	15.12.1990
Marital state	Gift, med ett barn (5 år)

Work experience

3/2018-today — **Shop assistant at Dagligvarer AS**
Various shop work where I was responsible for unpacking of goods, refilling in shelves as well as working as a checkout assistant

9/2014-3/2018 — At home with a small child whilst studying Norwegian

9/2017-6/2018 — **Røde Kors**
Voluntary work, organising courses at Røde Kors

Education

8/2015-today — **Speak Norsk, Oslo**
Norwegian courses, level B2, social studies

8/2010-6/2012 — **XYZ secondary school in Syria**
Two years of secondary school

Courses

2017 — Certification, Datakortet Mini at Folkeuniversitetet

Languages

- **Arabic** — Native written and oral
- **Norsk** — Intermediate written and advanced oral

Other

Interests: Reading, cooking and music

References

Beate Nilsen, shop manager at Dagligvarer AS, tel. 99 99 99 99
Per Nilsen, administrator of courses at Røde Kors, tel. 99 99 99 99

3. Examples

CV – Yana Hussami

Adresse Kaosveien 13, 1200 OSLO
E-post yana.hussami@gmail.com
Telefon +47 999 99 999
Født 15.12.1990
Sivilstand Gift, med ett barn (5 år)

Arbeidserfaring

3/2018-i dag	**Butikkmedarbeider hos Dagligvarer AS** Allsidig butikkarbeid hvor jeg hadde ansvar for å pakke ut varer, påfyll i hyller, samt arbeid i kassen
9/2014-3/2018	Hjemmeværende med et lite barn, mens jeg samtidig studerte norsk
9/2017-6/2018	**Røde Kors** Frivillig arbeid med organisering av kurs hos Røde Kors

Utdanning

8/2015-i dag	**Speak Norsk, Oslo** Norskkurs, nivå B2, samfunnskunnskap
8/2010-6/2012	**XYZ ungdomsskole i Syria** Toårig ungdomsskole

Kurs

2017	Sertifisering på Datakortet Mini hos Folkeuniversitetet

Språk

Arabisk	Flytende skriftlig og muntlig
Norsk	Godt skriftlig og meget godt muntlig

Annet

Fritidsinteresser	Lesing, matlaging, musikk

Referanser

Beate Nilsen, butikksjef hos Dagligvarer AS, tlf. 99 99 99 99
Per Nilsen, kursadministrator hos Røde Kors, tlf. 99 99 99 99

CV – Bilan Amburo

Address	Kaosveien 13, 1200 OSLO
E-mail	b-amburo@gmail.com
Telephone	+47 999 99 999
Birth date	15.12.1987
Marital state	Married with three children (3, 5 and 7 years old)

Work experience

3/2018-today	**Cleaner at EFG skole** Daily and periodic cleaning
9/2017-today	**Voluntary work at Røde Kors** Cooking and miscellaneous cleaning work at a Language cafe
9/2014-3/2018	At home with small children
3/2012-9/2014	Caretaking of sick parents

Education

8/2015-today	**Speak Norsk, Oslo** Norwegian classes, level B2
8/2010-6/2012	**XYZ secondary school in Somalia** Secondary school, two years

Courses

2017	Norwegian driving license class B for car with manual gears

Languages

Somalian	Native written and oral
Norwegian	Intermediate written and advanced oral

Other

Interests:	Cooking, children and caretaking

References

Kari Olsen, operational leader cleaning at Drammen kommune, tel. 99 99 99 99
Line Jansen, manager at Røde Kors language cafe, tel. 99 99 99 99

CV – Bilan Amburo

Adresse	Kaosveien 13, 1200 OSLO
E-post	b-amburo@gmail.com
Telefon	+47 999 99 999
Født	15.12.1987
Sivilstand	Gift, med tre barn (3, 5 og 7 år)

Arbeidserfaring

3/2018-i dag	**Renholder på EFG skole** Daglig og periodisk renhold
9/2017-i dag	**Frivillig arbeid hos Røde Kors** Matlaging og forefallende renhold på en språkkafe
9/2014-3/2018	Hjemmeværende med små barn
3/2012-9/2014	Omsorgsarbeid for syke foreldre

Utdanning

8/2015-i dag	**Speak Norsk, Oslo** Norskkurs, nivå B2
8/2010-6/2012	**XYZ ungdomsskole i Somalia** Toårig ungdomsskole

Kurs

2017	Norsk førerkort klasse B for bil med manuelt gir

Språk

Somalisk	Flytende skriftlig og muntlig
Norsk	Godt skriftlig og meget godt muntlig

Annet

Fritidsinteresser	Matlaging, barn og omsorg

Referanser

Kari Olsen, driftsleder renhold hos Namsos kommune, tlf. 99 99 99 99
Line Jansen, daglig leder for språkkafe hos Røde Kors, tlf. 99 99 99 99

3.5   Testimonial sample

Sample content

Bella Smith, born on 23.07.1988 was employed as an event manager with ABC from 01.01.2012 until 01.06.2015.

In this role, Bella was responsible for planning and setting up events arranged for various international groups. This work included planning the agenda and inviting speakers from academia and businesses all over the world. For each event Bella would send requests for abstracts and invite the speakers.

Bella was also responsible for updating the website and all other printed material for the events, as well as handling the practicalities – everything from ordering the venue, assisting with accommodation and ordering food and refreshments and so on.

Bella is a person who will take responsibility for new tasks with passion and spirit. She is hardworking, flexible and team-oriented, and I am sorry to see her leave our company.

I would highly recommend Bella Smith and wish her the best of luck!

***

If you are asked to write your own testimonial, you should write something like the first three paragraphs of the example above, while the last two paragraphs are examples of what the employer would add before signing the document. Your future employer will not know that some of the content was actually written by you.

The finished document in a Norwegian version is shown on the next page, so that you can also see the suggested layout.

3. Examples

Trondheim, 15.05.2015

ATTEST

Bella Smith, født den 23.07.1988, har vært ansatt som koordinator for ABC sine seminarer fra 01.01.2012 til 01.06.2015.

I denne rollen var hun ansvarlig for planlegging og igangsetting av arrangementer arrangert for ulike internasjonale grupper. Dette arbeidet omfattet å planlegge de ulike tema og finne forelesere fra universiteter og bedrifter over hele verden. For hvert seminar ordnet Bella med å innhente abstrakter og invitere foredragsholderne.

Bella var også ansvarlig for å oppdatere websiden og alt annet trykt materiale for seminarene. Hun håndterte også alt det praktiske, som for eksempel å finne konferansier, bestille lokaler, bistå med overnatting, bestille mat og forfriskninger og så videre.

Bella er en person som tar ansvaret for nye oppgaver med stort engasjement og vilje til å stå på når det trengs. Hun er en hardt arbeidende, fleksibel og en god lagspiller, og det er trist at hun nå skal slutte hos oss.

Jeg vil gi Bella Smith min alle beste anbefaling og ønsker henne lykke til videre!

Bedriftslogo

Med vennlig hilsen
for ABC

[signatur]

Kari Nordmann
Administrerende direktør

3.6 Statements to be avoided

These are statements which should be avoided in your application letter, CV and in the interview. This kind of bragging will most probably have a negative effect on the employer:

- I was the top student of my class
- I am the best
- I am a professional
- I am an excellent programmer
- My skills are outstanding
- I am a perfect fit for the job
- I am superior at creating networks and business connections
- I am 100% efficient in creating excellent marketing strategies
- I have exceptional analytical and organisational skills
- I have perfect problem-solving abilities
- I am able to handle any kind of problem
- I am a highly successful tech sales professional
- I am a dynamic & accomplished professional
- I am confident and successful
- I am extremely charming

If you were the top student of your class and you have a certificate to prove this, you could just include this when you submit copies of your certificates, without stating it in your application letter or CV. If you point out this fact in your documents or during the job interview, it may sound boastful and may therefore create a bit of distaste for the Norwegian interviewers. If you do decide that you want to mention it, it will probably sound a bit better to Norwegian ears if you say: '*I received an award for being the top student of my class*' – and only if you are able to document that it is true.

There is no good Norwegian translation for the term of being a professional. By using this expression in your job application you may come across to a Norwegian employer as a bit vague, as if you are trying to sound a better than you really are by using a non-descriptive term.

Instead I would recommend that you say what profession you are in, for instance: I am an engineer, architect, web developer or similar.

Remember that a job application is a formal document, and use of 'SMS language' (by using abbreviations like 'tech' and signs like '&' instead of 'and') like some of the examples above may give them the impression that you are a bit lazy.

Instead of writing that you are extremely charming, it would be better to write that you like to work with people.

You should also avoid telling them what to think or do, for example:
- You should invite me to a job interview
- I would like to be invited to a meeting where we can ...
- I have a friend who should be invited to an interview for the other vacant position

3.7 Examples of good statements

- I am an experienced IT professional with a broad background

- I have worked for four years with management and improvement of IT systems

- I have been responsible for contract negotiations, transitions and implementations

- I have worked with delivery of global services with in-house and outsourced services

- I was responsible for consultancy within service delivery and management

- I was responsible for developing and conducting courses

- I like to work with people

- I think it is very rewarding to have a job where I would get the possibility to help others.

As you will have seen by now, your own competence and personal qualities should be presented in matter-of-fact way in Norway. If you want to sell or promote yourself, it should be done in a more modest or subtle way by using the statements mentioned in chapter 2.1.

One important key to success is self-confidence.
An important key to self-confidence is preparation.

Arthur Ashe

4 THE JOB INTERVIEW

Congratulations! You have been invited for a job interview! You are a winner! Yes, you should consider yourself a winner if this happens, as whatever follows from now on will be exciting, informative and educational for you.

Even if you do not get the job you should think of the interview as useful practice. You will know and feel it when you make mistakes, but you will learn from them. As a result you will be better prepared next time and will not make the same mistakes. It takes practice to give a good performance at a job interview.

It is therefore very useful to have experienced some job interviews before the really important one for the dream job. I have a friend who applied for some jobs he did not really want, when he thought he would have a fair chance of being invited for an interview. He did this just to get some practice from job interviews, in order to learn from the kind of questions they might ask and so on.

When you have been called for an interview, it means that you are considered qualified for the job. In other words, you have something the employer wants, and being aware of this may help boost your confidence before and during the interview.

Since most job interviews are about distinguishing between formally qualified applicants, the focus will often be more on soft skills rather than academic or professional qualifications. The main objective will then be to get to know you better in order to establish how well you will fit into the workplace. These personal qualities often trump formal skills in the final selection of candidates. The focus on informal skills may come as a somewhat surprising experience to many foreign job seekers.

The report 'The art of fitting in' (21) confirms that personal qualities count for as much as 80 percent. Since every candidate interviewed is technically considered qualified for the job, the focus of the interview will often be on other qualifications, such as the soft or social skills.

The employer will try to assess whether you have the motivation they are looking for. Since the personality and attitudes often count for more than professional skills, it is important to try to establish a good chemistry with the recruiters, by showing genuine interest in the job - a 'sparkle'. This has to come across to them as natural, so it is always best to be yourself and try to relax as much as possible.

Other things such as your clothes, interests and leisure activities may be useful in finding out who you are to assess how well you will fit into their workplace. For example, if you are wearing something they consider inappropriate for an interview, they may think that you will also dress inappropriately for important meetings.

4. The job interview

4.1 Preparations

You should continue your research about the employer and position by checking on the internet and using your own network. You could also check the social media profiles of friend's and connection's to find out if any of them work there.

You should also look for good questions to ask during the interview, and learn the Norwegian words for professional terms within your area of competence.

I would advise that you practice your part aloud to hear yourself saying what you think you may say during the interview. By rehearsing aloud, you will hear it when you say something wrong or if your response sounds clumsy. If you only practice inside your own head, you will not hear your own mistakes as well as if you speak aloud. It is, of course, best to practice in front of another person who can give you criticism and feedback on how you convey the message. I recommend that you practice by answering the typical interview questions in chapter 4.3.

You should think of the job interview as an oral exam where you must be able to answer the questions in a professional and coherent way, without a lot of stuttering. Presenting yourself to a future employer is harder than you may think, but you can just try and see how well it goes.

Follow the company dress code. It may be worth your while going to the company at 4 PM to see what their employees are wearing when they leave work.

You should wear something neutral and semi-formal, however this will depend on what kind of job it is. You should, if possible, avoid wearing any religious symbols, caps, visible tattoos, noisy patterns, or anything else that might be distracting for the interviewer, or considered as unprofessional. Bearing in mind the Norwegian tendency to conform (Janteloven), you should also be careful of appearing glamorous or looking as if you have dressed for a party rather than work. Examples of things to avoid are short skirts, deep cleavage, too much perfume or jewelry as well as stiletto heels.

The outfit should however be something you feel comfortable in, so that you will not feel even more nervous and awkward. I therefore would advise that you decide on your outfit and try it on the day before to ensure that it still looks good on you.

Finding your unique selling points

Find advantages for recruiting you. This is very important, and you should ask yourself: 'Why should they recruit me? What are my unique selling points?'

Do you have some special competence that they need? Do you have any personal qualities that fit well with this position? Can you offer new ways of thinking or new skills, or can you add to the diversity in this organisation?

Try to think how you could turn your cultural background into an advantage. For instance, you could say that you come from a hard-working culture, and therefore you do not mind hard work, or that you have a hard-working attitude. Many Norwegian employers have experienced that not everyone in Norway, sadly, is hard-working anymore.

For example, if you are applying for a job as a nurse caring for old people, you could say that, in your culture, you are brought up to show respect for old people. Sadly we have lost some of this respect for elders in Norway. Bear in mind however, that you should only say these things if they are true.

It is important to use examples, and as part of your preparations for the interview, I would suggest that you prepare an example or a short story to elaborate upon each of your skills and personal qualities. They should ideally be situations where you have succeeded in something, but you could also use some where you have failed and learned something useful.

I would therefore recommend that you make a personal job application database with a collection of such examples, so that you will have something to select from during the interviews. If you have prepared some examples, you will sound more professional and convincing.

4.2. The interview

Bring the job advertisement with you, as well as the originals and copies of your other documents (i.e. your application letter, CV, certificates, testimonials and anything else you think might be relevant). If the employer has not received copies of your documents, you then have the option to leave behind any documents, in case they should ask for them.

You should allow time for the unexpected to happen on the way to the interview. The interview is a bit like an exam, where you will not be admitted if you arrive too late. As a recruiter in Norway, I would not employ somebody who did not arrive on time for the job interview.

I would advise that you plan to be there one hour early, so that you can check where the building and the correct entrance are. After you have found this out, you can look for a cafe nearby to have a cup of coffee, and a final read of the job announcement, your application letter and your questions. In this way you can calm your nerves a bit by being more focused before arriving five minutes early.

The employers will also notice what is not said, so you should pay attention to your body language. A firm handshake makes the best impression in Norway. Make sure you have eye contact with the person(s) during the interview, try to look calm, and remember to smile. Also make sure that you sit up straight in the chair, and that you lean forward a bit. Avoid sitting with your hands folded or in front of your chest, as this may make you look a bit defensive.

After shaking hands with the recruiters, the interview will probably start with a presentation of the company and the organisation you are hoping to work in.

After they have given you this information, they may ask you to give a short presentation of yourself. Here you should briefly summarise who you are, and what background you have. This will be followed by a dialogue between you and the interviewer(s) where they will ask you questions and you will have the opportunity to ask your own.

At the end of the interview they will probably tell you a bit about how the process will be from then on. Interviews usually take between 30 minutes and two hours, with 60 – 90 minutes being the most common.

During the interview, it is important that you show an interest in the company and the position. It is also a good idea to take notes, as it is an effective way of showing interest, and will help you to remember what is being said so that you can come up with follow-up questions later in the interview.

Show your motivation!

During the interview, you should constantly bear in mind that the most important thing is for you to convince them that you are genuinely motivated for this positon.

Language during the interview

If you speak some Norwegian, you could speak it at least in the introductory part of the interview.

I would advise however, that the moment it starts to become difficult for you to explain properly about yourself and your own competence, that you ask if it is ok to switch to English, because you can do a much better job at explaining these things in a more familiar language. Doing this is much better than stuttering away in Norwegian.

4.3 Selling yourself at the right level

During Norwegian job interviews, it is important to sell yourself at the right level. By overselling, you will cause suspicion and dislike. You should also bear "Janteloven" in mind.

Norwegians are brought up to be quite modest about their own achievements. Bragging is not part of the culture in Norway, even in job interviews. If you brag about your own competence and/or personal skills, it would be perceived by most Norwegians as overselling, and it would sound overconfident and cocky.

As mentioned in chapter 2.1 it may be difficult in Norway to find the right way of convincing a future employer that you, with your competence and personal qualities, are a good fit for the job. It is best to promote your own achievements in a more subtle and indirect way.

Also during the interview you could say: "I like..." or "I enjoy...". The interviewers will know that whatever you like doing, you do well.

Another way is to use statements like: "Other people say..." or "I receive good (or excellent) feedback on my work as..." Referring to what other people say sounds better than saying what you think about yourself.

You should bear in mind however, that your future employer might contact your references and ask them questions related to what you have said in the interview, and also about what "other people say" about you.

Teamwork is appreciated in Norway. Any big talk from you will be especially distasteful if it sounds like you are trying to take credit for the work of others, or downplay the contribution of other people.

If you say positive things about your colleagues and their role in your work, it will sound good because it shows that you are a team-player. By doing this, you will also give them the impression that you will be a positive contribution to their work environment, which is very important for them.

Some employers may have experienced foreign workers requiring more supervision than those who grew up in Norway. If you feel that you are able to show initiative, take responsibility and work without close supervision, it may be worth mentioning during the interview, but only if it is true.

4.4 Discussing your strengths and weaknesses

Be prepared to tell them about your strengths. Employers like candidates who are able to describe themselves as responsible, creative, flexible, a team-player, cooperative, and who likes challenges. You should ensure that your answers are honest, however. Your future employer may also talk to your references, so you should try to think what your references will say about you. Remember to have examples ready.

You may also be asked to tell them your weaknesses, which may be disguised as "What do you need to develop further?" or "What are your areas for improvement?" They will expect you to come up with something, as nobody is perfect. Again, you should think of what your references will say. Give examples and tell them how you plan to improve these.

If possible, you could talk about your weaknesses in a way that positions them as advantages if seen from another perspective. You should refrain from sounding too good to be true, though. Nobody is perfect, and if you are unable to talk about your own weaknesses in a thoughtful way, the employers will not be convinced that you are sincere.

4.5 Questions asked by employers

These are the questions you should rehearse aloud the answers to before the interview. There are links to more interview questions in the reference section (14).

- How would you describe yourself?
- How would other people describe you?

4. The job interview

- How would you describe our company?
- What made you move to Norway?
- How long do you plan to stay in Norway?
- Briefly describe your free time interests or hobbies
- Why did you apply for this position?
- Why do you want to change jobs?
- What motivates you at work?
- What does it take for you to perform optimally at work?
- What did you like the most (or least) in your previous job?
- What do you know about our company?
- Why do you think you are the right candidate?
- How do you handle conflicts?
- How do you handle stress?
- How do you like working as part of a team?
- What motivates you in a job like this?
- What would you start by doing in this job?
- Where do you see yourself in 3 (or 5) years from now?
- What has been your best achievement in your previous job(s)?
- What would your expectations be of us, as your employer?
- What is important for you when you are looking for an employer?
- What are the characteristics of a good (or bad) leader?
- How could you contribute to a good working environment?
- What question were you most afraid that we would ask during this interview – and why?
- What questions do you have for us?
- If we offered you this position, would you say "yes"?
- What are your salary expectations?

Be prepared to explain your answers with examples or short stories from your previous jobs or your private life. For instance, if you are asked about how you handle stress, you should be able to describe a stressful situation that you were in and how you handled it. The same goes for how you handle conflicts – in that case, you could give them an example of a difficult relationship you have had and how you dealt with it.

With regard to how you like working in a team; you should be able to explain how you will be able to contribute to good team work.

Seeing yourself and the position that you would like to be in in three-to-five years from now is quite hard, and I would advise you to be humble. Saying that you will be the head of department or similar may make you come across as a bit too competitive, and this is therefore probably not a good idea. Instead, you may say that three or five years is quite a long time, and that you would like to learn as much as possible, so that you can hopefully become an important contributor in the workplace.

The question of whether you will answer "yes" if they offer you the job may be a final check to see how motivated you really are for this particular position. If you need time to think before answering, they will perceive you as less motivated than if you answer unconditionally "yes" without any hesitation. So, unless during the interview you have already decided that you do not want the job, you should therefore answer unconditionally "yes" without hesitation. If and when you are formally offered the job, you will always be able to review the job offer and possibly decide not to accept it.

Salary expectations

If you are asked what your salary expectation is, you could tell them what you are earning today, and that you are hoping for a bit more in the new position.

If you are unsure what your expectations should be, I advise that you are honest and tell them that you are unsure, and then you can ask what the salary level is for this position. By doing this they will tell you what to expect, which will also give you an idea of what the salary level would be for similar positions for someone with your experience.

Not all employers will ask about your salary expectation. Some jobs are regulated by tariff agreements, in which you would be paid according to the tariff for someone with your background and experience. Positions in the public/governmental sector in Norway are also regulated, and the salary levels for these jobs are listed in the announcements. By studying these job announcements, you will learn a bit about salary levels in

Norway. However, the wages and salaries in the private sector are different from the government sector, and have more variation.

Speaking of salary, it might also be useful for you to know that bonus incentives in sales positions are less common in Norway than in many other western countries.

You should not negotiate salary during the interview, because the employer has not yet decided who they want for the position. If you start to demand higher salary at this point, it may reduce your chances of getting a job offer. You may be able to negotiate the salary when you have been offered the position. I will revert to this topic in chapter 6.4.

4.6   Questions you could ask

Norwegian employers will expect you to ask questions in the interview, and they usually allow time for this towards the end. If you do not take this opportunity however, they might perceive that you lack interest and are not motivated for the job.

Your questions could be along these lines:

- Assuming that I get the job, what do you think I should focus on to succeed?
- What would you as my leader expect from me?
- What kind of decisions would I be making in this position?
- What would you say are the biggest challenges of this job?
- What are the biggest challenges for your team?
- What would you say is the most important factor for a positive contribution to a good working environment in your team?
- Is there any reading material that you would recommend I read to get more information about your company?
- Could you please tell me how the process will be moving forward?

It would also be good if you could ask follow-up questions based on the presentation they gave you at the beginning of the interview.

4.7 Cases to test your skills

In some interviews you may be tested on your skills, by being asked by the employer to solve practical cases. Here are some examples, where in most instances you will be given a computer and an allotted amount of time, in which to complete the tasks:

- You are asked to find some relevant information on the internet. This information could be something that would be used by the employer in a given situation.

- You are given a request from a customer and are asked to draft a reply to them.

- You are asked to organise some practical details and meetings for your boss whilst travelling to a seminar in another country.

- Your boss receives an invitation to speak at a local event in another town in Norway. Answer the email and ask for any information you think might be useful for your boss, and which will also help her decide whether to attend the event or not.

- You are asked to write a letter or text in a language which is not your native tongue, to test your written language skills.

- You are responsible for 10 underage persons on a study trip to another country, and you are also their travel guide during the trip. Upon your return to Norway, you arrive with the group at the airport to find that all the tickets have been cancelled by a mistake. What would you do?

You may also receive one or several cases prior to the interview. The purpose of this is to test how you solve a task when you have had time to prepare. Make sure you allow enough time for preparations of the cases, as people who are well prepared usually perform better in solving them. In such a case, you should also consider whether to make a written presentation that you can show during the interview.

You may also be asked to take a language test, in order to establish what level your Norwegian language is at.

4.8 What else to be prepared for

Often there will be two people conducting the interview – usually the department manager and somebody from the HR (Human Resources). In some cases, there will be a panel with more than two person. Try to have most eye contact with whoever is asking you the questions, and some with the others also. They may be important decision-makers even if they are not saying anything.

You may get fewer questions about your professional skills and more about you as a person, than you might in other cultures. This might seem a little strange, but they have seen from your CV that you have relevant education and experience. They will not ask about things they are already convinced of, but about things they feel they need to know more about. The focus of the interview will therefore likely be to find out a bit more about you as a person. It is therefore very common to ask the candidates about their interests.

Be prepared for them to ask about your private life too. If you have not written about children in the CV, they may ask about this. They may also ask what made you come to Norway and how long you plan to stay, as they may be a bit curious regarding whether you plan to stay in the country and the position.

Asking these questions is meant to be friendly from their side, as they want to evaluate the whole person, and see how you will potentially fit in with the rest of their team. Many employers want to maintain a good working environment, so even if Norwegians tend to segregate between business and private matters, they will probably make an exception from this during the interview.

Some questions however are not allowed in job interviews. Examples are political views, religion and sexual orientation. They should also only ask about pregnancy if the work is in an environment that could be dangerous for an embryo. There is a portal which answers questions about discrimination, but unfortunately only in Norwegian (13).

If you get a question that you think is too personal, then you may ask them how it is relevant to the position. However, in order to be perceived as an open and positive person, you should try to answer if you can.

4.9 Cultural aspects in the interview

Any lack of formality during the job interview should not mislead you into thinking that the interviewers are without any real power, as this is not usually the case in Norway. Some of them may introduce themselves with only their first name, but they may still be important decision-makers. Norwegian interviews may have an informal and relaxed atmosphere, but it is still very important that you show motivation and interest in the position.

In Norway, it is perceived as positive and welcoming to smile during the interview. Humour may also be a good thing if it sounds natural and does not become too much or forced.

If, as a sign of respect, you are used to avoiding eye contact, you should be aware that doing this will create a negative impression and may spoil you chance of getting the job. It is therefore important to maintain eye contact, as mentioned earlier in this chapter.

Remember that interviewers are trying to find out if you are genuinely motivated for this particular position. You can do this by showing initiative during the interview, i.e. ask questions related to what they tell you and not only the pre-rehearsed ones. Try to sound confident without being arrogant.

You should avoid sounding too good to be true by overpromising or not being able to reflect upon your weaknesses. They will appreciate that you are yourself and show sincerity. Be careful with how you sell yourself and avoid statements such as the ones listed in chapter 3.5.

They may also ask you what you know about the company, its history and the recent press coverage. There may be some small talk where they are really testing your general knowledge of Norwegian society, and the top news in the Norwegian media lately, to see if you are following the local and domestic news.

There may also be some questions to test how well you fit into a Norwegian workplace, such as:

- Tell us about the last time you had to work independently to solve a challenge.

- Tell us about a mistake you made and how you handled it.
- When your leader asked you to do something you had a problem with (or did not agree with), what did you do?

My previous book, **Working with Norwegians**, explains in detail what Norwegian employers expect. Owing to Norway's harsh climate and sparse population, farms and villages were historically, and sometimes even today, cut-off from one-another due to snow and avalanches in winter. As such, people had to master several skills to survive, and some of this still prevails today. For example, Norwegians will often fix things in their homes and gardens themselves, and most shopping centers in Norway sell tools and equipment for this.
If we transfer this to the workplace it means that Norwegians tend to be generalists where they will work quite independently, and often take a wider responsibility without being instructed what to do.

In short, if these questions are asked, they will expect you to be able to work independently, and admit / learn from your mistakes. You are also expected to address any issues you may have with your leader.

You may bring some notes where you have written down some good questions. It is important to listen to what they say so that you do not ask about things that they have already explained.

Be yourself and sincere. If you are very nervous, you can tell them so. You will come across as sincere and they may let you get away with a some mistakes, due to your nervousness.

Avoid criticising your past employer(s) or colleague(s). This will just reflect badly on you, and they will become skeptical as to whether you will be a positive contribution to a good working environment.

Do not interrupt the interviewers. Interrupting is considered rude in Norway and may spoil an otherwise good impression.

Be prepared for the interviewer(s) to take small pauses during the interview. These pauses may actually be very positive – i.e. a sign of having made an impression on them, and that they need to reflect and let it sink in. Try to relax, and avoid the urge of filling in the pauses with nervous chatter!

Norwegians also tend to say "yes" whilst breathing in, when listening to others talking. Although it might sound like they have asthma or breathing problems(!), this is merely a cultural quirk, and most of them will be unaware that they are doing this. It is therefore quite natural that they will do this whilst you speak, and there is nothing to worry about.

You will usually be offered something to drink before the interview starts. If so, I would recommend accepting so that you can bring it with you. That way, if you are asked something that you are unsure how to respond to, you can 'buy' yourself some extra time by taking a sip before answering.

In Norway, everyone is expected to clear up after themselves in the workspace. So if you accepted the cup of coffee/tea or glass of water, take the empty cup or glass with you when you leave and ask where to put it. Make sure you take all your notes and papers with you.

When you finish the interview, you may ask if you can call in a couple of weeks' time to get some preliminary feedback. If however they say that they would prefer you not to, then you should respect the answer.

Life is 10% what happens to you and 90% how you react to it.

Charles R. Swindoll

5 WHAT EMPLOYERS LOOK FOR

In the report 'The art of fitting in'(21), some employers express that their ideal employee is someone who will take the lead yet remain humble, and who is independent, but knows their own limitations.

5.1 Selection of candidates

Hiring someone in Norway is like an investment, often with a high financial and organisational cost attached. This is because it costs money and effort for the organisation to train new people in processes, routines, use of technical equipment, etc.

There is also the element of strong job protection in Norway. With the exception of making people redundant due to financial difficulties, it is in most sectors quite hard to discharge an employee who is on a permanent contract. It is therefore vital to find the right candidate for the job.

It is equally important to recruit candidates who are likely to stay in the job for some time. Hiring people who leave after only a short period is a bad investment.

The employer will therefore evaluate your education, experience and personal qualities to try to establish how your competence is relevant for the position and the company.

The most important factors for employers are:

1. Your ability to deliver (professional skills)
2. How you will fit in with the rest of the team (personality)
3. If you will stay in this position (motivation)

1. Professional skills: Your ability to deliver

Employers will listen to how you describe your professional achievements and how you are able to reflect upon your own competence, to see if you are on the 'same page' as them.

They will evaluate if you are able to understand the challenges in the job, and try to find out if you have succeeded with similar tasks in your previous jobs. Even if your experience is not exactly what they are asking for, it could still be relevant. For instance, if you are applying for job as a consultant and you have previously worked as a teacher, you have probably gained some valuable people skills from the role that you could use as a consultant.

They will also try to establish if you are motivated for all the tasks of the job, and not just the more interesting ones.

Employers will try to find out what your attitude is to learning new things, in order to assess how much effort it will be to train you for the new position. Many organisations undergo frequent changes, and so they may also evaluate your willingness to adapt.

You should always bear in mind that they will consider the realism of what you say, and if you are able to deliver what you promise.

2. Personality: How you will fit in

The study 'The art of fitting in' (21) indicates that, in addition to the candidate, the workplace itself plays an important role in the job interview. Employers often make generalisations about the workplace culture, which is the environment where they would want you to fit in.

The employer's assessment of the workplace culture sets a standard that they will apply when you are evaluated as a candidate for a position in their organisation.

Having a good working environment is important for most employers, so they will want to find out what you are like as a person, to try to get a picture of how you will fit in with, and influence the rest of the team.

They may be curious about how you work in a team and might also be interested in how you describe the role of your colleagues in your work achievements.

It will be positive if you show an interest by asking relevant questions. Recruiters will observe how you relate to them; if you get a good connection, and if you show initiative during the interview session, by speaking to them not only when you are asked something. Showing initiative is appreciated in Norway, as in most jobs employees are expected to be able to show initiative and work without close supervision.

They will also observe your body language, such as eye contact, how you sit, and how you speak to them. They will look for small signs to convince them that you are honest and sincere.

3. Motivation: If you will stay in this position

The employer will want to be convinced that you understand what the job entails and that you are genuinely motivated for all the tasks, including the less interesting ones. The interviewers will observe your body language and your attitudes – in short your entire behaviour – to consider whether you have the 'sparkle' that is needed to stay in the job over time.

They might also evaluate whether the position has enough challenges for you to want to remain in it in the long-term. If they think you are overqualified for the job, it might be a challenge for you to convince them why you would stay.

I mentioned in chapter 4.4 that you might be asked what made you move to Norway and how long you plan to stay. They may be a bit curious as to whether you plan to stay in this country – and this position.

They will examine your CV to see if you have changed jobs very often. If you have had several positions where you have spent less than two years in each job, then it will probably create some uncertainty. If this is the case for you, you should be prepared to answer questions about it during the interview. Be careful criticising previous employers or colleagues as this could backfire on you and give them the perception that you are a quarreler, which is something they will not want in their organisation.

'Gut feeling'

Many Norwegian employers say that 'gut feeling' plays an important role when they select their candidates. The report 'The art of fitting in' (21) describes how employers have a great deal of freedom to emphasise personal suitability in the selection of candidates, and that the employers also feel very confident about trusting their own intuition.

5. What employers look for

The researchers also found that, after the interview, employers often could not remember what the candidate had said. On the other hand they remembered very well if the candidate had given them a good or bad feeling

It is therefore vital that you manage to convince them that you are motivated for this position. It is also very important that you do not pretend to be something you are not. I advise that you are sincere and convincing, and try to establish a good chemistry with the interviewers.

***

In my career as a recruiter I once turned down the candidate with the best professional qualifications for my team because I felt she would not make a positive contribution to the work environment. So even if she, from a purely technical point of view, had the best competence, I chose the second candidate on the list because my gut feeling told me that he would be a better team-player on our projects.

I had a well-functioning team with motivated people who supported each other in their daily tasks, and to me it was important that everyone contributed in a positive way to the work environment.

5.2   Results from an employer survey

Based on the survey *Ideas2evidence, Employer survey* (15), these are the prioritised competencies/qualities that employers look for':

1. Ability to collaborate
2. Ability to acquire new knowledge
3. Independent and critical thinking
4. Communication skills, written and oral
5. Ability to use skills in new areas
6. Ability to establish a network and build relationships
7. Academic and theoretical knowledge
8. Analytical skills
9. Ability to work under pressure
10. Methodological skills
11. Ability to manage and coordinate tasks

After studying this list, you might consider how any of these elements are descriptive of you, and how you can use them when you describe your personal qualities in the application letters and job interviews.

Doubt kills more dreams than failure ever will.
Suzy Kassem

6 GETTING STARTED IN NORWAY

6.1 The easiest ways into the job market

You should bear in mind that Norway is a very egalitarian society, and that showing a will to work will be highly valued by employers.

As mentioned earlier, voluntary work has a high value since it shows that you are a person who cares for others. Working for a voluntary organisation will also give you a Norwegian reference.

Having a temporary job is a good (and much easier) way of getting into the job market. Most Norwegian employers will think it is much better that you have had a low paid/status temporary job than no job at all, because this shows that you are willing to work.

If you are in a temporary job, you may get access to the internal job market within the organisation. When they know you and your qualities, they may find that you are a very good candidate for permanent positions within the company. More about this in the next chapter.

Another option is to look for jobs outside the town centers. In the larger cities in Norway, it is often much easier to get a job in the outskirts if you are willing to commute a bit.

It is generally much easier to get jobs in northern Norway. Because many Norwegians have moved to the south, there are many vacancies left in the north; everything from medical doctors, nurses, dentists, teachers and fisheries. Living in the north may not seem so tempting at first glance, but people in northern Norway are known for being much more open and hospitable towards people they do not know. Socialising and making friends in Norway might therefore be easier in the north.

In southern/western Norway, it is generally a bit easier to get jobs in fisheries.

The health sector all over Norway seems to have a constant need for nurses and medical doctors, even if the need is highest in the northern parts. These professions are regulated in Norway (18), but there are still possibilities to work as temporary workers within care for elderly people whilst waiting for the Norwegian authorisation.

Schools and kindergartens are in constant need of temporary help, but recruiters are becoming stricter with the Norwegian language requirement for people who want to work there.

Restaurants often struggle to get enough chefs and waiters. As such, some restaurant owners have begun travelling abroad, in their endeavors to recruit chefs that they are now unable to find in Norway.

Hotels also struggle to get all the staff they need, so working as a night receptionist or chambermaid is one way of getting into the Norwegian labour market.

Being a driver is another possibility. Although taxi driving is quite restricted by the governmental license system, there are other driving jobs available.

It is also relatively easy to get jobs within construction and maintenance in Norway. Until recently these jobs were very popular amongst Poles, however many have started moving back to Poland.

6.2   A possible door opener for the dream job

Temporary jobs are an important part of today's labour market. If you find it difficult to get a permanent position, you should definitely consider temporary work whilst looking for your dream job. It is often much easier to get a temporary job than a permanent position, and working as a temp can actually be just as beneficial to you as a permanent position. It is unrealistic to think that you will get your dream job right away, and therefore it is better to start in a temporary or a different type of job than you originally intended. Starting a working career in a temporary position has many benefits, and is more than just an income whilst waiting for something better to come along:

Useful work experience

In Norway, there are many job-seekers with higher education, but they lack experience. Most employers place an emphasis on work experience when hiring. A temporary job can be a golden opportunity to gain a foothold in the labor market. If you are a recent graduate or newcomer to Norway, it is important to get started in the job market.

Work experience is never wasted and even a short-term temporary job may give you useful experience. You should therefore never rule out temporary jobs too quickly. A temporary position will help you build up work experience in Norway, at the same time as you will get Norwegian references. This will most likely make you more attractive to future employers – including your dream employer.

Access to an internal labour market

As a temporary worker, you will be on the inside of the company and get information about vacancies that are only advertised internally. And even for positions that are advertised externally, since you already work for them, you will have shown what you are capable of. This can give you an advantage over external candidates. It is quite common for temporary workers to eventually get permanent employment.

An easier way to get into Norwegian workplaces

It is often much easier to get a temporary position than a permanent one, but temporary jobs are often underestimated by job-seekers. For example, as a barista or waiter, you will meet a lot of people, and you will get to practice Norwegian. You will become accustomed to providing service and relating to different people, and you may also learn some administrative tasks. These are skills that employers in all industries ask for. It is therefore valuable experience that you can benefit from later, and you can add it to your CV.

Network and new opportunities

By working as a temp, you will get a unique opportunity to build networks. You will learn about different industries and possible future professions. Your career is created whilst working, and your dreams may change many times during the process. Maybe you want to try something new, but are unsure of what would suit you best. A temporary position can be a perfect opportunity to get to know yourself by finding out what you enjoy doing and what you are good at.

Do not be afraid to take a job you are overqualified for

Even if you are overqualified for a job, it is important to be open for opportunities. Instead of waiting for the dream job, you should focus on getting valuable work experience. Many Norwegian employers say that they have respect for candidates who have shown that they are willing to make an effort. It is much better to have had jobs you are overqualified for, than giving them an impression that you are a person who is without work due to lack of initiative.

Flexibility and freedom

A temporary position can also provide more flexibility and freedom in your daily work. For example, you can combine a temporary job with studies or childcare. Whilst in a temporary job, you can still actively explore new challenges.

***

If you lack experience in Norway, it is a good idea to take a temporary job to get started in your career. In fact, it may be crucial if you want to reach your goals. In a temporary position, you will get an introduction to Norwegian work life, at the same time as you will become familiar with your own skills. You will also get an insight into what is in demand in the labor market. Then, all of a sudden, new and exciting opportunities that you did not even dream about may appear.

6.3 Some final advice

As mentioned at the beginning of this book, you should make an effort to learn the language. Most companies prefer to hire Norwegian speakers, as this will be the easiest option for them. In addition to the language barrier, being able to speak Norwegian probably means that you can more easily understand how Norwegian workplaces function, so many of them will perceive this as the 'safest' option.

Even if the employer does not require you to speak Norwegian, you will always feel a bit left out in the workplace when your colleagues speak Norwegian in meetings or by the coffee machine and so on. Some people will prefer to speak their native language in their native country, and will feel that it is their right to do so. There is no way you are going to be able to change that.

The employers who will accept English speakers are in academia and technology oriented companies within information and communication technology (ICT), engineering, oil, gas, energy and gaming industry. Some hotels, bars, restaurants and shops will also accept English speakers. In other industries it will vary more from place to place.

If possible, you should ask Norwegian friends or acquaintances for help with your application letter and CV, since they will not only be able to help you with the language, but may also have some contacts. In addition, they may be able to give you some tips based on their own experience and how the system works in Norway. If your Norwegian is on a basic level you could try to make the application letter in Norwegian, with some help and quality checking from a Norwegian friend. In such a case the CV could still be in English, since you are not a fluent Norwegian speaker.

It is also possible to send open/general applications, or walk around to employers of interest to deliver them in person. If it is a small employer, you may be able to speak to the manager, and hand your application directly over to him or her. In bigger places you could try to ask to talk to the staff in the personnel office or HR department, but they will usually have a reception where you would probably have to hand over you documents to the receptionist.

Open applications should still be tailored as much as possible to the company where you are applying. You should also include an application letter explaining what kind of job you are looking for and why you would like to work there.

I would recommend that you write that, if they do not have any openings at the moment, they keep your application until they have a vacant position.

I advised a friend from Ukraine to do this, and she walked around to several hotels in Bergen with her application letter and CV. In one of the hotels she met the manager, who told her that they had no vacancies at that time, however, the manager kept the documents. After some weeks my friend got a call from the manager who said that they had got a good impression of her, and she was invited for an interview. Afterwards my friend was offered a part-time job. It was not in the reception as she had hoped for, but as a chambermaid with a potential for landing a job as a receptionist later. In addition, her CV would show that she was not afraid of hard work by taking a job as a chambermaid, which would look good for a future Norwegian employer.

You should, however, be prepared for no response from such employers since they do get many people calling on them in the hope of getting a job, so it is not easy.

Norway is a country based on networking, and networking is in fact one of the most important ways of getting a job (17). You should use your network in Norway for all it is worth. Tell people that you are looking for a job and ask their advice. Use social networks, such as LinkedIn, Twitter and Facebook. Your connections may be door openers into new networks for you, and tips may often come from remote connections.

Check LinkedIn and Facebook for connections and friends who work for employers that you would like to work for. Connect your LinkedIn CV to Twitter and Facebook. Follow headhunters on Twitter and #hashtag your professional field.

There are several examples in Norway of people who have landed their dream jobs by posting very untraditional and creative posts on Facebook (16).

In addition to the job portals and links mentioned in chapter 1, there are also job announcements in local newspapers and magazines.

You can also check the homepages of employers of interest. Many of them will announce job vacancies on their websites, and some have an online system where you can register your CV. I would recommend that you include an application letter explaining why you are motivated for working for that particular employer. Here you could also ask them to keep your application until they have a vacant position that fits your profile.

Expect your future employers to check your digital footprint by searching your name on the internet. Do a search for your name to see what comes up that a future employer may find. You should also browse the photos associated with your name. Maybe something should be deleted?

I have a friend who has a 'namesake' with the same name as him who has published some very bad things on the internet. During job interviews my friend always informs the employer that this person with the same name as him, is in fact another person.

Low-volume hiring seasons

The months of June, July and August, as well as December and January are generally quiet seasons for announcing vacant positions and hiring new personnel.

Since many Norwegians take their main holidays in July, which is called 'fellesferie', work life in Norway more or less takes a break too. Most employers will therefore avoid announcing vacant positions during the period around 'fellesferie', until they have full manpower again.

In December there is a tradition for Christmas preparations and celebrations, and many businesses will work at reduced speed. In addition, it is relatively common for many organisations to have to wait some weeks (sometimes even months) in the new year to have a full overview of their budgets, for new or temporary posts.

Employers therefore prefer not to hire new staff in the period around July and December.

Because the hiring process can take a long time, there are usually fewer vacant positions announced in June, July, August, and in December and January.

Now that you are aware of these facts, you may decide to make other plans, relax and do other things, or take a vacation during these periods.

6.4 Getting the job offer

When you have completed the final interview, the process may still take several weeks or even months before you hear anything. The employer will first send a job offer to the candidate on the top of the shortlist. Only when the first candidate has accepted the job offer and signed the contract, will the rest of the candidates be informed that they did not get the job.

If the top candidate declines the job offer, it will be sent to the next one on the list, and so on, until one of the candidates has accepted the job and signed the contract. While this goes on, all the other candidates will be kept waiting. It may therefore take several weeks or months even before you hear anything, especially in large organisations.

You are entitled to a written employment contract for permanent or temporary jobs in Norway. Make sure you understand all the terms and conditions for the job, how your payment is calculated, as well as how and when you will be paid.

It is common to have a probation period for permanent positions in Norway. The length of the probation period will be in the contract, with a maximum of six months. If you fail to deliver or do not live up to your employers expectation, they can normally terminate your contact with 14 days' notice during this period. This does not happen often – and usually only in severe cases, so it is nothing to lose sleep over.

Most job offers have a deadline for acceptance of the position, from one day to several weeks. It is important to sign and return the agreement before the deadline. If you need more time because you are waiting for another job offer, you should contact the employer and ask for the deadline to be extended. This may spoil some of the good impression you made in the interview, and you will probably need to give a reason for your request. You can either be honest, or you can say you need more time to read and understand the contract properly, or that you have some clarifications to make.

Assistance with finding accommodation

If you are getting a job offer and need accommodation in Norway, you may ask your future employer if they can help you find some accommodation.

Some employers are able to provide an apartment on a short or long term temporary basis for newcomers to the city/country. Even if they are not able to provide a flat for you, they may be able to give you some advice on how and where to look.

Getting into the house rental market can also be challenging in the large cities. This is outside the scope of this book, but I suggest that you ask your future employer and network for advice.

6.5   Salary negotiations before accepting a job offer

Once you have been offered the job, you may have an opportunity to negotiate your salary. You have this opportunity now – in the case of salary adjustments at a later stage, it is usually more difficult to negotiate, and it may take several years for you to catch up if your salary was in the low range to begin with.

You have the possibility to have a discussion with the employer to negotiate payment in a meeting, by email or in a phone conversation. It is best to do this quickly, so that the employer can consider your salary request before the deadline for accepting the job expires.

Before any salary discussions, you should become familiar with salary statistics (ref. chapter 6.8 about trade unions) for the position which you have been offered. You should also try to have an idea about your own 'market value', based on such things as whether you have other (especially better paid job options), how experienced you are and whether you fill all the requirements in the job announcement.

Whatever strategy you choose should depend on how confident you are that the employer wants you to fill the position as well as how interested you are in this job, and how important it is for you to be better paid. You could reply that you would really like to have the position, provided that you get a specific salary level, however you must then be prepared for the offer to be passed on to the next candidate in their shortlist. If this will be your first job in Norway and you have no other job alternatives at hand, it will be important for you to get started in a position as soon as possible. In such a case I would advise to be careful discussing salary, unless it is obvious that it is too low.

Other conditions that may be negotiable in addition to salary are having your costs reimbursed for relocation, mobile phone, wifi connection in your home, time off arrangements (*avspaseringsordninger*), education, as well as the ability to work part of the time from home.

If after you have been employed, you feel that your salary level is too low, you may still request that your salary be re-evaluated at the next yearly salary regulation, but normally you will not be able to achieve as much as during the recruitment process.

6.6 If you did not get the job

If you were invited for one or several interviews but did not get the job, you should call the employer to ask what you should improve in the future. It is very common and perfectly fine to do this, and their input will be valuable for you for your next interviews.

Reflect upon what you could have done differently, based on the input from the employer as well as your own impression and 'gut feeling' from previous interview(s). Be open and discuss it with your friends and network to see if they have any tips for you, based on their own experience and your particular situation.

Relax for a few days and do something enjoyable to revive your energy and put you in a better mood before writing the next application. Bear in mind that you were invited for the interview, so you were very close to getting the job. You had something that the employer wanted!

If you were not invited for the interview, you should focus on further improvement of you application letter and CV. Everybody knows that it is hard to get a job, especially the first one, so it should not be considered a defeat to have submitted several unsuccessful job applications, or been unsuccessful at several interviews. I suggest that you are open about it and share your experience with people you know.

Alexander Graham Bell said: *"When one door closes another door opens, but we so often look so long and so regretfully upon the closed door, that we do not see the ones which open for us"*. So you need to move on and start looking for other opportunities.

The closed door situation happened to me: This book would not have been written and my company, Ellis Culture, would not have existed if one door had not closed for me. Today I am really pleased that things turned out the way they did.

Or put another way:

> *Remember that not getting what you want is sometimes a wonderful stroke of luck.*
>
> Dalai Lama

6.7 Starting your own business in Norway

If you want to start your own business in Norway, you may find a lot of useful information from the Company Information Service and from the webpage Spør-oss (19).

You may also contact the local office for commerce and trade (Næringsetaten) in the municipality where you will live. They will give you information on how to proceed.

New companies in Norway are registered online on the Brønnøysundregister webage (20). This is a fairly simple process if you already know the name of the company and what kind of a company you are going to register (usually a sole proprietorship or a private limited company with shares).

There are also some organisations that provide information, courses and support for entrepreneurs.

You should check out Etablerersenteret and Innovation Norway on these pages:

Etablerersenteret.no
Innovasjonnorge.no/en

6.8 Trade unions

A trade union is an association of workers within a professional group. Trade unions play an important role in Norwegian working life, and it is a legal right and fully acceptable to join one. Being a member is very common, but not mandatory, and most employers regard unions positively. If your employer does not want you to join a union, it may be a sign that they do not have serious/proper intentions towards your employment. Equally, they will be aware that unions may be able to provide you with protection from being exploited at work.

The trade unions are working for good salary and working conditions, safety and your co-determination in case of changes to your work environment. They fight for issues such as: employment contract, working hours, holidays, education, equality, leave of absence and retirement schemes. They also engage in the development of rules for health, environment and security which will provide safety and adaption of the workplace.

The trade union representative represents you as an employee and may assist with problems with working conditions, wages and similar. As a member of a union, you become stronger because you are with others, and you also make others stronger by joining. You will be part of a larger network and you can contribute to developing the conditions in the workplace.

Many non-Norwegian employees in Norway do not see the value of a union membership. However, if you are not a member, you may not benefit when negotiations of salary and work conditions take place. In addition you will not have the support of the unions in case of any issues or problems in the workplace. You may also miss out on information, because employers will often use the unions as information channels towards the employees.

It may be a good idea to ask for a meeting with the local union representative to ask for information on how they operate and what the benefits are. They will usually appreciate you demonstrating such an initiative.

Trade unions are also good sources of information, and some publish magazines advertising vacancies in their industry.

In addition to being a source of information, membership in a Norwegian union does offer some benefits. Many unions offer career advice, training and courses, as well as help to quality-check your employment contract.

They can also give you access to statistics that will enable you to evaluate how your salary compares with others in your sector, industry and region. They will also assist with juridical questions and provide support if your contract is terminated or you are unemployed. Union membership may also give you some discounts on insurances, banks and other things such as hotels and fuel. There is a fee to be a member of unions, and this fee is tax deductable.

These are the most important confederations of trade unions in Norway:

LO – The Norwegian Confederation of Trade Unions

This organisation can give you an overview of the various trade unions in Norway, depending on the sector you want to work in.
www.lo.no

UNIO

This is Norway's second largest trade union confederation. Their members work in teaching, nursing and the police.
www.unio.no

Akademikerne

This is a confederation of professionals with higher education.
www.akademikerne.no

YS – Yrkesorganisasjonenes Fellesforbund

This is a large union confederation consisting of 23 federations covering different employment sectors.
www.ys.no

7 PERSONALITY TESTS

Personality tests are fairly common in the private industry and less common in the public/governmental sector and academia.

They will usually take place after the first or second interview, where you will be asked if you are willing to undergo such tests. If you want the job, you would need a very good excuse to be able to say no.

Sometimes there may be a case presented during the interview which you are asked to solve.

7.1　Why personality tests are used

Many employers think that the most important thing in the recruitment process is to avoid employing the wrong candidate. For example, one that does not fit into the organization or one that does not develop or perform as expected.

There is strong job protection in Norway, so once somebody is employed it is in many sectors quite hard for an employer to terminate a contract. The exception is when the employer has to reduce manpower due to a financial crisis, reduced sales or similar.

In Norway, there is a high threshold for firing people. Making mistakes in your job is normally not reason enough to be discharged, unless you keep on making the same mistakes repeatedly and are not showing any willingness to learn or improve.

It is not very common to fire people during the trial period either. Many foreigners in Norway are nervous of what will happen at the end of the trial period. Although the trial period should be considered as a test, you should not lose any sleep over it. If you show a good attitude and that you are eager to learn, there should be no reason why your contract would not be converted to a permanent one.

When I worked as a manager in a large Norwegian company I once tried to fire someone during the trial period, but was stopped from doing so by someone in the HR department who told me that the trial period was only a matter of form, and that it was now up to me to do a better job of following him up. When I left my position and moved on to another job, he was still there…

In summary, employment is an investment for the company and it is therefore extremely important to find the right candidate. In many cases, salary will be paid whether the person is performing or not.

7.2 Types of tests

The tests can be divided into three main categories:

1. **Personality analysis** – where they will test your:
   - Ability to cooperate
   - Loyalty and outwardness
   - Emotional stability and empathy
   - Creativity and energy

2. **Capability tests** – which are similar to the so-called IQ tests

   - Numerical, verbal and creative ability
   - Intelligence tests
   - Measuring of skills

These two types of tests will take place in a controlled environment, often on a computer, within an allotted time.

3. **Simulation tests or cases**

These are comprehensive exercises or assignments where you are asked to solve and prioritise job related tasks. The exercises may be critical job situations to be solved with other participants, organised as a miniature project. Your behavior will be evaluated, both on an individual basis and as a team member.

These kinds of tests are more common when several candidates are recruited at the same time, e.g. for a trainee programme or similar, where the other participants in the project group may be other candidates on the employer's shortlist.

7.3 Tips for the tests

The most important thing is to keep your concentration levels up, and to be honest. Focus on one question at the time and shut everything else out. For the personality analysis test, the first answer that comes to mind is in most cases the best. You should let your intuition guide you and try to keep calm. By doing this you will be able to answer honestly and quickly without stressing too much.

If you try to stop and find what you believe is the most 'correct' answer for the employer, your dishonesty will be revealed in similar questions later. Another revealing factor is that you will not make enough progress in the test, and will therefore be unable to answer as many questions in the allotted time.

Keep up the pace without stressing, and stick to the order without jumping back and forth in the test. Jumping will slow you down and give you a lower score, and it may also confuse you, producing unexpected and unwanted results.

Make sure that you answer the right question. This may seem like a silly statement, but when in a stressed situation, it is easy to tick off on the wrong line. I would therefore advise you to bring something that you can use as a ruler, in case the questions are arranged such a way that this might happen.

I would also advise you to practice by taking some tests. If you do, you should imagine that the questions are asked in a job context to get a consistent result.

Some of the results might surprise you and trigger some useful reflection. Maybe there are some parts of your personality that you were not aware of. This might be useful in gathering knowledge about yourself, as mentioned in chapter 1.2.

Your score results may be increased significantly by practicing and improving your technique.

This practice can be compared with puzzling the Rubik's cube, where each face must have only one colour for it to be solved. The more you practice, the quicker you are able to get all the colours in the right place.

By practicing, you are able to improve your results in personality tests in the same way.

Free personality tests

Typical personality tests are available on the internet, here are some examples:

- www.outofservice.com/bigfive (English)
- www.humanmetrics.com (English)
- www.careerfitter.com (English)
- www.assessment.com (English)
- www.careerfulfillment.com (English)
- wonderlictestsample.com/50-question-wonderlic-test (English)
- www.cebglobal.com (English)
- www.jobbsafari.no/persontypetest (Norwegian)

You could also just do an internet search for 'Free online personality tests'.

*Anyone who has never made a mistake
has never tried anything new.*

Albert Einstein

CLOSING NOTE

I would like to close this book now by wishing you the best of luck in Norway and with job-seeking in particular!

Thank you for reading my book! I hope you have enjoyed it, and that it will help you with your job-seeking endeavors. If you want to learn what to expect as a newcomer in a Norwegian workplace, I recommend my book **Working with Norwegians** which is also published in Norwegian under the title **Kunsten å arbeide med nordmenn**. It can be ordered from my website **www.ellisculture.com**, from the **Ellis Culture** Facebook page, or from Amazon.

Please feel free to contact me if you have any questions, challenges or input related to applying for jobs in Norway, and I will try to help you the best I can. I like to have a dialogue with people from all over the world as it gives me inspiration in my work, and I learn a lot from it.

If you have any suggestions regarding how this book could be improved, then I would like to hear them. As this is the first edition, it could probably be extended with more topics and other improvements.

If you are on Facebook and like the **Ellis Culture** Facebook page, you will be updated about cultural issues in or about Norway.

Courses/workshops/lectures

If you are able to gather a group of people who would benefit from a session of *Working with Norwegians* or *Applying for a job in Norway*, then it would be my pleasure to conduct training on demand.

I also develop and conduct training for diverse environments, such as ***Working in a multicultural environment***, ***Leadership of a multicultural environment*** and ***Exploring Cultural Diversity.***

The courses and workshops can be conducted all over the world.

You can contact me at: **ellisculture@gmail.com**

You may find more information on my webpage: **www.ellisculture.com.**

Bergen, 14th May 2018

Karin Ellis

REFERENCES

1. ManpowerGroup
   manpowergroup.no/Presse/MEOS-Q1-2018-Sterkeste-arbeidsmarkedsutsikter-pa-fem-ar/

2. NAV EEA Unemployment Benefit (EEA Administration):
   Telephone: +47 21 07 37 00   e-mail: eos@nav.no

3. NAV
   www.nav.no
   www.nav.no/workinnorway/

4. NAV Bedriftsundersøkelse:
   www.nav.no/no/NAV+og+samfunn/Kunnskap/Analyser+fra+NAV/Arbeid+og+velferd/Arbeid+og+velferd/bedriftsunders%C3%B8kelsen

5. NAV Service Center Eures
   eures@nav.no

6. NAV Tutorial
   mylittlenorway.com/2011/08/finding-a-job-on-nav-tutorial/

7. Less immigration to Norway
   nrk.no/sognogfjordane/svakaste-veksten-pa-13-ar-_-mindre-innvandring-og-faerre-fodslar-1.13930811

8. NOKUT webpage
   www.nokut.no/en/
   www.nokut.no/en/surveys-and-databases/list-of-industries/
   www.nokut.no/en/application-services--foreign-education/recognition-of-foreign-higher-education/#_3
   www.nokut.no/utdanning-fra-utlandet/Realkompetansevurdering/
   www.nokut.no/soknader--utdanning-fra-utlandet/godkjenning-av-utenlandsk-fag--og-yrkesopplaring/
   ww.nokut.no/soknader--utdanning-fra-utlandet/godkjenning-av-utenlandsk-fagskoleutdanning/

9. Research about photo on CV
   forskning.no/arbeid/2010/12/pent-bilde-ingen-fribillett

10. Research about jobseekers with foreign names
    Statsvitenskapelig tidsskrift, 25 (4): 307-329 2009 Midtbøen, A & Rogstad, J: «Diskrimineringens art, omfang og årsaker» I: Søkelys på arbeidslivet, 25 (3): 417-429

11. Testimonial template
    http://www.dagensperspektiv.no/nyttig/maler/mal-for-attest

12. Portal for voluntary work in Norway
    www.frivillig.no

13. Portal about discrimination in the workplace
    http://www.ldo.no/en/diskriminert/arbeidsliv/

14. Link to interview questions
    biginterview.com/blog/behavioral-interview-questions
    blogs.hbr.org/2012/05/when_choosing_a_job_culture_matter.html
    blogs.hbr.org/schrage/2012/05/projects-are-the-new-job-inter.html

15. Ideas2evidence, Employer Survey
    uib.no/filearchive/kompetanse-2020-rapport-16-02-11-.pdf

16. Dream job after posting on Facebook
    facebook.com/photo.php?fbid=919726758159916&set=a.110247039107896.12708.100003678008103&type=3&theater

17. Corruption vs. network in Norway
    migrationofemotion.com/2017/06/11/corruption-vs-network-in-norway/

18. Regulation for Health care personnel in Norway
    helsedirektoratet.no/english/authorisation-and-license-for-health-personnel

19. Company Information Service
    www.bedin.no
    www.spor-oss.no

20. Brønnøysundregisteret
    www.brreg.no/home

21. Jon Rogstad og Erika Braanen Sterri:
    The art of fitting in. Employers' evaluations of job applicants
    www.idunn.no/tfs/2018/01/passe_inn_og_passe_til

22. Jon Rogstad og Erika Braanen Sterri:
    Kulturelt betinget naturlig beskjedenhet
    En studie av jobbintervjuets muligheter og begrensninger

23. Jon Rogstad og Erika Braanen Sterri:
    Passe inn og passe til
    Oppfølging og mestring blant nyansatte arbeidstakere

ABOUT THE AUTHOR

Karin Ellis is an IT engineer with 30 years of professional experience, and 20 years of leadership experience with large international companies. Some of the teams reporting to her were multicultural and distributed across several geographic locations.

Karin has lived and worked in several countries, and participated in many international projects, where she worked closely with people from around the world. As a result, she soon developed a strong desire to understand and learn more about other cultures. Karin has conducted systematic interviews with hundreds of people to gather information about the code of conduct and unwritten rules in different cultures.

In 2011, Karin decided to follow a new path and live out her passion in developing and conducting intercultural training. She started **Ellis Culture**, a company delivering practical, job-related courses with specific tips on how to achieve better communication with members of other cultures. The practical exercises in the courses are taken from Karin's own experiences in multicultural environments.

In 2012, Karin was asked to develop the ***Applying for jobs in Norway*** s training course for a large Norwegian university. This book is based on the content from this course.

In addition to being the Chief Executive Officer of Ellis Culture, Karin has been the Honorary Consul of Estonia in Bergen since 2014.

Printed in Poland
by Amazon Fulfillment
Poland Sp. z o.o., Wrocław